ESSENTIAL

Evidence

by

Tracey Aquino, LLB, Barrister
Lecturer in Law
South Bank University

First published in Great Britain 1997 by Cavendish Publishing Limited, The Glass House, Wharton Street, London WC1X 9PX

Telephone: 0171-278 8000   Facsimile: 0171-278 8080

Aquino, Tracey
Essential Evidence
1. Evidence (Law) – England 2. Evidence, Criminal – England
I Title
344.2′056

ISBN 1-85941-145-2

Printed and bound in Great Britain

For Kate, Lucy, Beth and James

Foreword

This book is part of the Cavendish Essential series. The books in the series are designed to provide useful revision aids for the hard-pressed student. They are not, of course, intended to be substitutes for more detailed treatises. Other textbooks in the Cavendish portfolio must supply these gaps.

Each book in the series follows a uniform format of a checklist of the areas covered in each chapter followed by expanded treatment of 'Essential' issues looking at examination topics in depth.

The team of authors bring a wealth of lecturing and examining experience to the task in hand. Many of us can even recall what it was like to face law examinations!

Professor Nicholas Bourne
General Editor, Essential Series
Swansea Law School

Table of contents

Insanity

If the defendant wishes to argue that he is innocent because he was suffering from insanity at the time of the offence, then he bears the legal burden. This is because a man is presumed to be sane, and to know the nature of his actions: *M'Naghten's Case* (1843).

This only applies to insanity within the narrow definition in *M'Naghten's Case*; if a defendant raises non-insane automatism, he has no legal burden of proof: *Bratty v AG of N Ireland* (1963).

If the defendant raises insanity he only has to prove it on the balance of probabilities. If the prosecution raises the issue of the defendant's insanity then the prosecution bears the legal burden of proof, and must prove this disputed point beyond reasonable doubt.

Express statutory exceptions

Parliament is sovereign, and can thus place the legal burden on the defendant if it sees fit. This usually occurs in cases where it would be very onerous if the prosecution had the legal burden and where policy dictates that it should be on the defendant.

Such statutes tend to use phrases such as 'it shall be for the defence to prove' or 'unless the contrary is proved'.

Common examples include:

- diminished responsibility (s 2 Homicide Act 1957), where the defendant must prove that he was suffering from a defect of reason that impaired his responsibility;
- possession of offensive weapons (s 1 Prevention of Crime Act 1953), where a defendant in possession of an offensive weapon must prove lawful authority or reasonable excuse;
- possession of controlled drugs (s 6 Misuse of Drugs Act 1971), where a defendant has the legal burden of proving that he did not know or suspect the substance to be cannabis.

Statutes which imply the burden

A statute will contain a definition of the offence that it creates and the usual rule is that the prosecution bears the legal burden of proving all the contentious issues, including disproving any defence raised. However, it is possible that one of the areas in dispute is an issue that can be properly categorised as 'an exception, exemption, proviso, excuse or qualification'. The defendant may then bear the legal burden of proving that point, as the burden may be implied on him by reference to s 101 Magistrates' Courts Act 1980.

Section 101 Magistrates' Courts Act 1980

Section 101 is a restatement of an earlier statutory provision, which is in turn a statement of the then existing common law: *R v Edwards* (1975). As such the principle applies to all criminal trials, regardless of whether they take place in the magistrates' or Crown court.

Section 101 provides:

Where a defendant ... relies for his defence on any exception, exemption, proviso, excuse or qualification ... the burden of proving ... shall be on him.

This is regardless of whether the exception, etc appears as part of the enactment creating the offence, or whether it appears as a positive or negative requirement.

The essence of s 101 is that it can apply where a statute prohibits certain behaviour unless there is some explanation or excuse for the defendant's behaviour that the statute recognises. If this is the true construction of the statute then it may be possible to imply that Parliament intended the defendant to bear the legal burden of proving the explanation or excuse, as an exception to the rule in *Woolmington v DPP* (1935).

Determining whether s 101 applies

In determining whether s 101 applies, and whether it is Parliament's intention to impose the legal burden on the defendant, it is necessary to look at 'the mischief at which the Act was aimed and practical considerations affecting the burden of proof, and, in particular, the ease or difficulty that the respective parties would encounter in discharging the burden': *Nimmo v Alexander Cowan & Sons* (1968).

The mischief of the Act

In *Nimmo* the House of Lords based their consideration of who bore the legal burden on whether it was reasonably practicable to make the workplace safe in a case where the plaintiff had been injured at work. The House of Lords had to interpret s 209 Factories Act 1961, which could impose civil and criminal liability.

It was decided that the legal burden was on the defendant, who was in effect relying on an excuse for the workplace not being safe. This gave effect to the aim of the statute, which was to protect employees in their working environment. It would be easier for the defendant to discharge the burden. The defendant had the knowledge of his resources and the awareness of safety precautions available in his industry, all of which would be difficult if the plaintiff in a civil case, or the prosecution in a criminal case, were given the legal burden.

Exceptions must be set up by those who rely on them

In *R v Edwards* the Court of Appeal considered who bore the legal burden in a case where the defendant was accused of selling alcohol without a licence. Clearly the prosecution bore the burden of proving the sale of alcohol, but the dispute was as to where the burden lay in respect of the issue of licence. The court held that the burden was on the defendant by implication.

There was no basis for the argument that a defendant only bore the burden if the facts were within his sole knowledge. Instead the defendant bears the burden for 'offences arising under enactments which prohibit the doing of an act save in special circumstances or by persons of specified classes or with specified circumstances or with the licence or permission of specified authorities'.

Thus it is for the defendant to show that the special circumstances exist, or that he falls in the specified class or circumstances or has the licence or permission specified.

The true construction of the statute

It is important to remember that it is the true construction of the statute that leads to the conclusion of who bears the legal burden. It is not just a question of looking at the words used.

This was stressed by the House of Lords in *R v Hunt* (1987), where the statute prohibited the possession of controlled drugs, but regulations provided that the prohibition did not extend to mixtures containing less than a particular percentage of morphine. The legal burden of proving the composition of the mixture was on the prosecution. On a true construction this was not within s 101.

How onerous is the burden?

The House of Lords stressed in *R v Hunt* that Parliament would not intend to impose too onerous a duty on the defendant: 'When all the cases are analysed, those in which the courts have held that the burden lies on the defendant are those cases in which the burden can be easily discharged.'

This was a serious offence, with serious consequences for the defendant if found guilty. Any ambiguity should be resolved in favour of the defendant. It would be very difficult for him to have the substance forensically tested, whereas this would be easy for the prosecution.

The evidential burden

In a criminal case the prosecution bears both a legal and evidential burden. Whilst the legal burden is an obligation to prove a point, the evidential burden is the obligation to raise a *prima facie* case, ie enough evidence on which a reasonable tribunal could convict, thereby establishing a case for the defendant to answer: *Jayasena v The Queen* (1970). If the prosecution fails to discharge the evidential burden then the defendant will succeed in making a submission of no case to answer at the end of the prosecution case. If the prosecution succeed in discharging the evidential burden, then they can be said to have 'passed the judge' and justified the leaving of the case to the jury.

The defendant does not usually bear a legal burden of proof in a criminal case, but he will often have an evidential burden. If the defendant wishes to do more than merely deny the prosecution case, and wishes to raise an affirmative defence, then he will bear the evidential burden of raising this defence. To succeed in discharging this burden, he must 'lay a proper foundation' (*R v Cottle* (1958)), or 'raise the issue in a genuine fashion': *R v Carter* (1959).

Thus a defendant must do more than just assert a defence; he must provide some evidence in support of it, in order to justify the defence being considered by the jury. Once he has discharged the evidential burden, he will not usually bear the legal burden of proving his defence. The prosecution usually have the legal burden of proving disputed issues in criminal cases (*Woolmington v DPP* (1935)), and so the prosecution will need to disprove the defence raised.

In the following cases the defendant has the evidential burden to raise enough evidence in support of his defence to justify the defence being considered seriously by the jury, whilst the prosecution have the legal burden of disproving the defendant's defence:
- drunkenness (*Kennedy v HM Advocate* (1944));
- provocation (*Mancini v DPP* (1942));
- self-defence (*R v Lobell* (1957));
- duress (*R v Gill* (1963)).
- non-insane automatism (*Bratty v AG* (1963)), where it is for the prosecution to prove the conscious commission of the crime by the

defendant, if the defendant manages to discharge his evidential burden by providing prima facie evidence of automatism: *Hill v Baxter* (1958);

- alibi (*R v Johnson* (1961)) held that it was a mistake to direct the jury that the defendant had the legal burden of proving his alibi). In *R v Preece* (1992) it was suggested that it was good practice for the judge to direct the jury on the legal burden of proof in such cases to avoid them being left with the impression that the defendant had the obligation to prove he was where he had said in his alibi;
- belief in consent in rape cases: *R v Gardiner* (1994).

The burden of proof where admissibility of evidence is challenged

The general rule is that the party tendering or calling the evidence bears the legal burden of establishing admissibility: *R v Thompson* (1893).

The standard of proof

The standard of proof is the degree of cogency required of evidence to satisfy the legal burden of proof. In criminal cases the prosecution must prove any issue for which they have the legal burden beyond reasonable doubt: *Woolmington v DPP* (1935).

In the exceptional cases where the defendant bears the legal burden, he need only prove the point on the balance of probabilities, which is a much lower standard: *R v Carr-Briant* (1943).

In *Miller v Ministry of Pensions* (1947), Lord Denning elaborated on what was meant by beyond reasonable doubt. He said:

It need not reach certainty, but it must carry a high degree of probability. Proof beyond reasonable doubt does not mean proof beyond a shadow of a doubt ... if the evidence is so strong against a man as to leave only a remote possibility in his favour which can be dismissed with the sentence 'of course it is possible, but not in the least probable' the case is proved beyond reasonable doubt, but nothing beyond that will suffice.

Judges have found it difficult to resist the temptation to provide further explanation of the phrase beyond reasonable doubt. It is not enough to use phrases such as 'satisfied' (*R v Hepworth and Fearnley* (1955)), but it would be acceptable to use 'satisfied so that you are sure of guilt': *R v Summers* (1952). It is the effect of the summing up that counts (*Walters v R* (1969)), where the judge likened the standard to the degree of certainty required in matters of importance in the jury's own affairs. However, this kind of unnecessary elaboration should be avoided, and a model direction is like that in *Ferguson v R* (1979) where the judge told the jury that they should be 'satisfied beyond reasonable doubt so that you are sure of the defendant's guilt'.

The standard of proof for admissibility

Where a party has the legal burden of proving the admissibility of evidence, then such admissibility must be proved beyond reasonable doubt if the burden is on the prosecution, but only on the balance of probability if the burden is on the defence (*R v Yacoob* (1931) – regarding competence of a witness).

Where a party tenders evidence, and the authenticity of such evidence is being disputed, then only a *prima facie* case of the genuineness or authenticity need to be made out in order for the evidence to be admissible: *R v Robson* (1972). It will then be for the jury to see if they believe the evidence.

The position is more complex when there is a dispute over the authorship of certain written material. Section 8 Criminal Procedure Act 1865 permits the disputed written material to be compared with other writing that the court is satisfied is the genuine work of a person. The standard of proof in relation to the genuineness of this other writing has been held to be on the balance of probabilities (*R v Angeli* (1979)), but this was criticised in *R v Ewing* (1983). In *R v Ewing* the court thought that in civil cases the balance of probability test was sufficient, but that if the burden was on the prosecution in a criminal case, then they should have to prove the genuineness of the other writing beyond reasonable doubt before it could be used as a comparison with the disputed material.

Civil cases

The legal burden of proof

In civil cases the parties are theoretically equals, and there is no need to routinely protect one party with the kind of general rule that exists in *Woolmington v DPP*. Instead in civil cases the legal burden lies according to the maxim 'He who asserts must prove'.

It will be necessary to look at the pleadings in any given case in order to see who bears the burden on a particular issue, and take into account the nature of the plaintiff's claim and the defendant's response to that claim.

In a basic civil case the plaintiff will assert the elements of his case, for example the elements of a tort or breach of contract. The plaintiff will then have the legal burden of proving his assertions and will have to establish a tort or contract that has been breached.

A defendant who merely denies the plaintiff's claim will have no legal burden. If, however, he raises an affirmative defence such as volenti or contributory negligence in tort, or an exclusion clause in contract, for example, then he will bear the legal burden of proving his defence.

In *Joseph Constantine Steamship Line v Imperial Smelting Corp* (1942) the plaintiff sued the defendant for breach of contract in not supplying the ship the plaintiff had agreed to charter. The defendant responded using the defence of frustration, since the ship had been destroyed by an explosion at sea. Frustration cannot be relied on if the defendant is at fault, and the case turned on who bore the legal burden in relation to the fault of the defendant. Clearly the plaintiff had the legal burden of proving the existence of the contract and its breach. By raising the affirmative defence of frustration the defendant had the legal burden of showing that performance of the contract was impossible. On the issue of fault it was held that the plaintiff bore the legal burden. Generally it is easier to prove a positive than a negative, and consequently it would be too onerous for the defendants to prove lack of fault.

In some cases, however, it may be too onerous for the plaintiff to prove an issue, and then the burden of proof can be placed on the defence. This happened in *Levison v Patent Steam Carpet Cleaning Co* (1948) where the plaintiff sued the defendant for breach of contract when the defendant lost a carpet that the plaintiff had entrusted to the defendant for cleaning. The plaintiff had the legal burden of showing a contract existed and that it had been breached. The defendants then raised an exclusion clause as an affirmative defence, which they clearly had the burden of proving, and this clause covered them if they were negligent but did not cover them if they were in fundamental breach. Since the carpet had been in the sole control of the defendants and the plaintiff had no way of knowing what had happened to his carpet, the defendants bore the legal burden of proving that they were not in fundamental breach.

Whether the issue relates to breach of contract or to the existence of a defence depends upon the construction of the contract in the particular case. In *Rhesa Shipping v Edmunds* (1985) the plaintiff claimed for breach of an insurance contract when the defendant insurance company failed to pay on the sinking of the plaintiff's ship. The plaintiff contended that the ship had sunk through a peril of the sea, ie being hit by a submarine, whilst the defendant argued the sinking was through wear and tear, which was not covered by the policy. The trial judge was not convinced by either version of events, but gave judgment for the plaintiff because their version of events was more likely than the defendants. The House of Lords held that this was wrong. Who wins the case depends upon who has the legal burden of proving how the ship sank. If the way in which the ship sank was part of the contractual terms and related to breach, then the plaintiff would bear the burden, and since the judge was not satisfied with the explanation of peril of sea, the claim would fail. If, however, how the ship sank was part of an affirmative defence, such as an exclusion clause, then the burden would be on the defendant, who would then lose if he did not convince the judge. On a true construction of this contract, it was a term that the defendant would pay if the ship sank through peril of the sea. The plaintiff had the legal burden of proving a breach of contract, and therefore the plaintiff had to prove that the ship sank through peril of the sea. Consequently the plaintiff lost their case.

The evidential burden

In civil cases the parties may also have evidential burdens, ie an obligation to raise enough evidence on an issue to justify the court considering the point. In civil cases there are usually no difficulties with the evidential burden as costs, penalties and procedural rules ensure that parties rarely pursue issues that cannot be backed by some evidence.

Admissibility of evidence

In civil cases, as in criminal cases, the party tendering the evidence has the legal burden of proving admissibility. However, the standard of proof is the lower one of the balance of probabilities.

Standard of proof

In civil cases the standard of proof for both parties is the balance of probabilities. This was explained by Lord Denning in *Miller v Ministry of Pensions* as 'more probable than not'.

However, civil cases can involve allegations of varying gravity and so if the allegation being made is very grave or serious then more evidence will be needed to tip the balance of probabilities. In *Hornal v Neuberger Products* (1957) the court held that in a civil case the standard of proof for breach of warranty was the same as that for fraud, ie the balance of probabilities. However, the court would need more evidence in order to be satisfied that fraud was more probable than not than it would if the allegation were one of breach of warranty.

In *Re Dellow's Will Trusts* (1964) the standard of balance of probabilities was applied to an allegation of murder being made in a civil case. The court stated: '... the gravity of the issue becomes part of the circumstances which the court takes into consideration ... the more serious the allegation the more cogent is the evidence required to overcome the unlikelihood of what is alleged and thus to prove it.'

It is also the case that allegations of sexual abuse of children, when made in civil proceedings, must be established on the balance of probabilities: *Re H and R* (1995).

In matrimonial cases the standard of proof for certain allegations used to be beyond reasonable doubt, to reflect the disastrous consequences that allegations of matrimonial misconduct used to have: *Bater v Bater* (1951). However, in *Bastable v Bastable* (1968) the Court of Appeal decided that the ordinary civil standard of proof was more in line with current views on divorce and matrimonial breakdown, subject to the Hornal comment that the graver the allegation, the more evidence would be needed.

The balance of probability test is also used in legitimacy cases to rebut the presumption of legitimacy in s 26 Family Law Reform Act 1969.

Presumptions

A true legal presumption is a rebuttable rule of law that operates once a party proves a primary fact or facts to presume a secondary fact is proven, even though no evidence on that secondary fact has been presented. The presumption can be rebutted by the opponent raising *prima facie* evidence to suggest that the secondary fact does not exist, ie discharging an evidential burden, in the case of an evidential presumption, some presumptions are more difficult to rebut. These are called persuasive presumptions and require the opponent to disprove the secondary fact, ie discharge a legal burden.

The main presumptions are validity of marriage, legitimacy, death and *res ipsa loquitur* at common law and ss 11, 12, 13 Civil Evidence Act 1968 and s 74 PACE 1984 at statute.

Other evidential rules exist that are false presumptions, such as recent possession of stolen goods, continuance of life, intention and incapacity of a child under 10 to commit a crime. (Detailed consideration of these rules can be found in *Lecture Notes on Evidence* by Alan Taylor, 1995, Cavendish Publishing Limited.)

2 Competence and compellability

You should be familiar with the following areas: ✓

- competence of the defendant as a witness for the defence, co-accused and prosecution
- competence of the defendant's spouse as a witness for the defence, co-accused and prosecution
- competence of children in criminal cases
- competence of persons of defective intellect in criminal cases
- competence of the parties, their spouses in civil cases
- competence of children and persons of defective intellect in civil cases
- oaths and affirmations

Introduction

Competence is the legal test of an individual's ability to testify as a witness in court. Compellability ensures that a potential witness can be forced to testify, even though they may be reluctant or unwilling to do so. In order to ensure that decisions are reached on the basis of the maximum amount of relevant evidence the general rule is that all witnesses are competent and compellable.

However, there are certain categories of witness where this general rule is modified. This may be because of concern over that person's ability to give reliable evidence, or because there are policy considerations that make a variation desirable. Policy constraints dictate that different rules should apply to a defendant and his or her spouse, whereas historically concern has existed as to the reliability of evidence given by children and the mentally handicapped.

The competence of a witness is a question of law for the judge to determine, and the burden of proving competence is on the party calling the witness.

The defendant

As a witness for the defence

It used not to be possible for the defendant in a criminal trial to testify in his own defence. His obvious interest in the outcome of proceedings arguably gave him an inherent unreliability, and the unenviable choice between lying or incriminating himself.

Section 1 Criminal Evidence Act 1898 renders the accused competent to testify in his own defence, but s 1(a) states that he is not compellable. This means that the defendant is free to choose whether or not to testify, and is sometimes referred to as the defendant's right to silence. Until recently the law took the view that if the defendant exercised this right to silence, then it was not open to the jury to infer that his absence from the witness box indicated his guilt: *R v Bathurst* (1968). This ensured the maximum protection for the defendant, and accorded with the principle in *Woolmington v DPP* (1935) that it is for the prosecution to prove the defendant's guilt, and not for the defendant to prove his innocence.

This position has been dramatically altered by s 35 Criminal Justice and Public Order Act 1994, which provides that adverse inferences can be drawn in appropriate cases from the defendant's failure to testify. This legislation was designed to give effect to concerns that silence was being used as a shield by guilty, and often very experienced and dangerous, criminals. Opponents, including the Royal Commission on Criminal Justice (Cmd 2263) and Lord Taylor, the Lord Chief Justice, argued that there was little statistical evidence to back claims that silence led to higher rates of acquittal, and that this represents a change in emphasis from protecting the innocent towards convicting the guilty.

Section 35 is of enormous significance, and must be read in the light of the Court of Appeal's Decision in *R v Cowan and Others* (1995).

The section applies to all defendants over the age of 14 who are pleading not guilty and who are physically and mentally capable of testifying. If counsel for the defendant does not inform the court that the defendant is testifying, then the judge must ensure, in the presence of the jury, that the defendant understands that he has the right to testify and that adverse inferences may be drawn if he does not do so: s 35(2) and the Practice Direction 1995.

This will occur at the end of the prosecution case and after the defendant has had the opportunity to make a submission of no case to answer.

Section 35(3) then provides that the court or jury can draw such inferences as appear proper from the accused's failure to testify or answer questions without good cause, although s 35(4) makes it clear that the defendant is not compellable.

In *R v Cowan* (1995) the Court of Appeal made it clear that s 35 is of universal application, and not limited to exceptional cases. Once the judge is satisfied that the prosecution has established a *prima facie* case for the defendant to answer, ie discharged their evidential burden, then he must direct the jury on the evidential effect of the defendant's failure to testify.

Firstly the jury are required to consider whether the prosecution have established a *prima facie* case to the satisfaction of the jury. The jury will be reminded that the defendant does not have to testify and that he has a right to silence, and that it is for the prosecution to prove his guilt.

It is then necessary to consider whether any evidence has emerged in the course of the trial to suggest that the defendant may have good reason for not testifying. It is not possible for counsel to merely suggest possible reasons, there must be evidence to back this. It will not be a good reason if the defendant has previous convictions that he is trying to prevent being revealed if his shield is lost under s 1(f) Criminal Evidence Act 1898. This requirement may make it difficult for defendants to show good reason, since a defendant who does not testify through fear is hardly likely to provide evidence of threats to him and his family!

If there is no good reason then the jury can draw such inferences as they see fit, including the inference that the defendant has no answer to the prosecution case, or none that would stand up to cross-examination. This means that the jury will be able to infer guilt from silence, although silence on its own cannot be enough for a conviction: s 38 Criminal Justice and Public Order Act 1994. The defendant's failure to testify in his own defence is an additional evidential factor in the prosecution case.

The judge and co-accused have always been able to comment on the defendant's failure to testify, but s 1 Criminal Evidence Act used to prohibit prosecution comment. This was altered by the Criminal Justice and Public Order Act 1994, and the prosecution can comment on such matters.

As a witness for a co-accused

The defendant is a competent but not compellable witness for a co-accused: s 1 Criminal Evidence Act 1898.

It is unlikely that a defendant would want to testify for a co-accused and not for himself, since that would expose him to cross-examination by the prosecution. In the past this issue arose where defendants testified at a *voir dire* for the benefit of a co-accused, but did not testify in the main trial. Since adverse inferences can now be drawn from a failure to testify in the main trial, this possibility is even more unlikely.

If a defendant ceases to be jointly charged with his co-accused then he is competent and compellable for the co-accused: *R v Boal* (1965). This could arise if the defendant pleads guilty, or the charges against him are dropped, or, more controversially, if there are separate trials: *R v Richardson* (1967).

As a witness for the prosecution

The defendant is not a competent witness for the prosecution, and cannot be called to testify for the prosecution either against himself or against a co-accused. Any conviction obtained by using an incompetent defendant is a nullity: *R v Grant* (1944).

The prohibition on the defendant testifying against a co-accused only applies whilst the defendant is still at jeopardy of being convicted for his own part in the offence. If he no longer runs the risk of being convicted then he will be competent and compellable for the prosecution. A defendant becomes competent and compellable if he pleads guilty to the offence, if the charges are dropped, or if he is acquitted on the direction of the trial judge.

If there are separate trials of the two accused then, as a matter of good practice, the prosecution should not call one accused to give evidence in the separate trial of the other unless they have indicated that the case against the accused witness will not proceed: *R v Pipe* (1967).

If an accused does become a competent witness for the prosecution, then he can be compelled to testify. He would be classed as an accomplice, and in the past judges were required to give a corroboration warning in respect of such evidence. However, there is no longer any need for a routine corroboration warning: s 32 Criminal Justice and Public Order Act 1994 (see Chapter 7). The judge will only tell the jury to be careful about relying on such testimony if there is evidence emerging in the trial that illustrates a cause for concern: *R v Makanjuola* (1995).

The spouse of the defendant

Special rules apply to spouses, ie to a person who is lawfully married to the accused. If the couple are cohabitees, the so called common law marriage, then they fall outside the special rules and are just treated as ordinary witnesses for the purpose of competence and compellability. If the marriage is invalid for any reason, such a polygamy in *R v Khan* (1986), then again the ordinary rules apply, and not the special rules relating to spouses. Consequently the cohabitee and party to a void marriage are competent and compellable.

Effect of divorce

At common law, once a marriage was ended by divorce, an ex-spouse could not testify in respect of events that occurred within the marriage. This position was altered by s 80(5) Police and Criminal Evidence Act 1984 which provides that on divorce an ex-spouse is competent and compellable in respect of events that occurred at any time, including events within the period of marriage. The same applies when a marriage is ended by nullity proceedings.

As a witness for the defendant

Section 80(1) Police and Criminal Evidence Act 1984 makes a spouse a competent witness for the defendant, and s 80(2) renders a spouse compellable for the defendant unless they are jointly charged, s 80(4). This gives a defendant the right to insist that their spouse testifies, even though the spouse may be reluctant to so so. However, there is no right to insist on a spouse testifying if the spouse is also accused with the defendant.

As a witness for a co-accused

Section 80(1) renders a spouse competent for anyone jointly charged with the defendant. However, where the defendant and the co-accused are charged in the same count on the indictment then the spouse of the defendant is not compellable for the co accused unless the offence falls within one of the special categories of offence in s 80(3).

These categories are:
* charges involving assaults, injury or threats of injury to a spouse or a person under 16;

- sexual offences where the victim is under 16;
- attempting, conspiring, aiding, abetting, counselling, procuring or inciting any offence that falls in the above two categories.

If the defendant and the co accused are being tried together, but are charged with separate offences on the same indictment, and do not appear in the same count on the indictment then the rule in *R v Woolgar* (1991) applies. This renders a spouse competent and compellable for the co-accused. The result has been criticised as adopting an inconsistent approach to s 80(1) and s 80(3) and ignoring the common law position, but it remains good law.

As a witness for the prosecution

Section 80(1) renders a a spouse a competent witness for the prosecution, unless the spouse is jointly charged: s 80(4).

However, a spouse is not usually compellable for the prosecution, and will therefore have a choice of whether or not to testify.

Section 80(3) renders a spouse compellable for the prosecution in certain cases that involve:
- assaults, injury or threat of injury to the spouse or persons under 16;
- sexual offences where the victim is under 16;
- attempting, conspiring, aiding, abetting, counselling, procuring or inciting any offence that falls in the above two categories.

This is a compromise position that recognises that whilst it may be undesirable to force a spouse to testify against their partner, in certain cases this may be the only way to protect the spouse or other vulnerable person, and it may also be the only evidence available to the prosecution.

The choice of whether to testify

If a spouse is not compellable then it is for them to choose whether or not to testify. They do not have to testify just because they have made a complaint to the police, made a statement or indicated that they would testify previously, *R v Pitt* (1983), and can exercise this choice up to the point of entering the witness box and taking the oath. Once they have taken the oath then the spouse must answer questions put to them, and cannot pick and choose which to answer.

Commenting on failure of a spouse to testify

If a spouse chooses not to testify then the judge and co-accused can comment on their failure to testify. The prosecution are forbidden from commenting by s 80(8) and this has not been altered by the Criminal Justice and Public Order Act 1994.

If the judge does comment he should be careful to avoid any suggestion that the spouse was under any obligation to establish the innocence of the defendant: *R v Naudeer* (1984). This is because the prosecution bears the burden of proving guilt and the defendant is not obliged to call evidence to establish his innocence. The jury have just been deprived of the opportunity of hearing the spouse's explanation. The same care should be taken about commenting on the failure of the defence to call other witnesses, such as co-habitees: *R v Weller* (1984).

Children

The evidence of children tended to be viewed with suspicion as it was perceived that children were prone to fantasising and were often inherently unreliable as witnesses. For these reasons the law used to impose strict tests before a child could be regarded as a competent witness, and even then it was considered necessary to insist on corroboration for the child's testimony.

However, the modern view is that a child's evidence should be more readily received, and that the child is not such an unreliable witness as had been thought. Provided that the child has been properly questioned during the investigation, and has not been pressurised or subjected to suggestive questioning, then its evidence will not be tainted. Through a number of statutory measures Parliament has altered the rules regarding children's evidence, and introduced procedural measures to ensure that testifying is as untraumatic as possible.

The child who is under 14

Unsworn evidence
Children who are under 14 at the time they testify must give unsworn evidence only: s 52 Criminal Justice Act 1991, inserting a new s 33A into the Criminal Justice Act 1988. There is no possibility of such a child giving sworn evidence, and there is no need for the child's unsworn evidence to be corroborated: s 34 CJA 1988.

The test of competence

Section 52(2) CJA 1991 attempted to apply the same test for declaring a child not competent to testify as that which was applied for all other persons. The intention was to ensure that children's evidence was more readily received than before, without any enquiry as to whether the child had the kind of understanding that used to be necessary for a child to take the oath.

The section was not clearly worded and consequently clarification was provided by Sched 9 para 33 of the Criminal Justice and Public Order Act 1994. This provides that a child's evidence shall be received unless it appears to the court that the child is incapable of giving intelligible testimony.

The effect of the new test

Older cases suggested that it was undesirable for very young children to testify: *R v Wallwork* (1958) which concerned a five year old child. However, the modern view is that much depends on the individual child, and that there is no reason why very young children, if properly handled, will be any more unreliable than other witnesses: *R v Z* (1990) which concerned a six year old child's competence.

Ruling on competence

The Home Secretary made it clear that judges should not hold preliminary interviews with the child, as such questioning tended to undermine and intimidate the child. Instead the child should begin to testify, with the judge only declaring the child incompetent if its testimony was unintelligible. This reform makes any enquiry into a child's understanding of the need for truth unnecessary and redundant.

In *R v Hampshire* (1995) it was suggested that the judge should form a view of the child's competence by viewing video recorded interviews involving the child which had been prepared for the trial under s 32A CJA 1988. Only if there was no such video, or if there was doubt should the judge conduct an investigation. This should be done in the presence of the accused, but in the absence of the jury, and should just involve the judge talking to the child, not any detailed legalistic cross-examination.

The child between 14 and 18

Sworn evidence

A child who is between 14 and 18 at the date of testifying can only give sworn evidence.

The test of competence

In *R v Hayes* (1977) it was held that the test of a child's ability to give evidence on oath depended on whether the child had sufficient understanding of the need for truth over and above the everyday need for truth and an understanding of the solemnity of the occasion.

At that time it was thought that children usually reached this level of understanding between the ages of 8 and 10. Clearly now that this test is only applicable to the 14 years and older child, it would normally be assumed that such a child was competent.

Ruling on competence

In most cases involving a child over 14 there will be no real problem on competence. It is only where the child is mentally retarded or educationally subnormal that there will be any doubt over his competence.

If competence is an issue it used to be tested by the trial judge in open court in the presence of the jury: *R v Dunne* (1929). However, if expert evidence is called as to the nature and extent of the child's disability, then this should be received in the absence of the jury: *R v Deakin* (1994). It now seems following *R v Hampshire* that all testing of a child's competence should be in the absence of a jury.

Persons of defective intellect

If an adult witness appears to be mentally handicapped or of defective intellect then it will be necessary to consider the witness' competence. The test to be applied, according to *R v Bellamy* (1985), is the *R v Hayes* (1977) test of whether the witness has sufficient understanding of the solemnity of the occasion and the need to tell the truth over and above the everyday duty.

Much will depend on the extent of the witness' handicap or mental impairment. The judge should carry out his questioning of the witness in open court and if expert evidence is to be presented, the jury should not be present: *R v Deakin* (1994). It may also be, following *R v Hampshire* that all enquiries into a witness' competence should be in the absence of the jury.

Miscellaneous categories

Sovereigns, heads of state and diplomats are competent but not compellable.

Bankers and bank staff cannot be compelled to give testimony in cases where the bank is not a party, nor can they be required to produce original bank books and records. Instead a copy of the records is admissible without the need to call bank personnel to verify the entries: Bankers' Books Evidence Act 1879.

Civil cases

The parties

The parties to an action are competent and compellable (s 2 Evidence Act 1851), and can in theory insist on calling each other to testify. This is rare, but happened recently in America when a publishing company subpoenaed its opponent, Joan Collins, to testify in a breach of contract case.

Spouses

The spouse of a party is competent and compellable to give evidence in civil proceedings: s 1 Evidence Amendment Act 1853.

However, an ex spouse is in an anomalous situation in that the old common law rule in *Monroe v Twistleton* (1802) has survived. This means that an ex spouse is not competent to testify about events that occurred within the marriage, and can only testify about events occurring before the marriage took place or after the marriage ended.

Children

In civil cases the rules (below) apply to children under the age of 18.

A child can give sworn evidence if he or she satisfies the *R v Hayes* (1977) test and understands the solemnity of the occasion and the need for truth over and above the everyday need. Case law would indicate that this level of understanding is usually reached between the ages of 8 and 10.

If a child does not have sufficient understanding to take the oath it can give unsworn evidence under s 96(1) Children Act 1989. The test is whether the child has sufficient understanding to justify the

reception of its evidence, and can understand the need for truth. It is submitted that this is the ordinary need for truth, not any greater need.

Persons of defective intellect

Such persons must give sworn evidence, and will only be competent if they satisfy the *R v Hayes* test of understanding the solemnity of the occasion and the need for truth over and above the everyday need.

Oaths and affirmations

Evidence at trial may be given on oath by swearing to tell the truth by reference to some divine body, or on affirmation, which is a solemn undertaking to tell the truth. It is for the witness to choose, and both are forms of sworn evidence and have equal weight, ss 4 and 5 Oaths Act 1978. Unsworn evidence is usually a nullity unless expressly permitted, as for example, for children, licensing and extradition proceedings, witnesses merely producing documents, and judges and counsel giving evidence about cases they were involved in.

3 Examination in chief

Calling witnesses

A party must decide which witnesses it wishes to call to testify. As a general rule there is no property in a witness, and either side can call the witnesses it wishes to, subject to competence and compellability criteria: *Harmony Shipping Co SA v Saudi Europe Line* (1979). In this case an expert could be subpoenaed by the defence, even though the expert had already given an opinion to the plaintiff. Obviously the contents of the report to the plaintiff were privileged and could not be revealed, but that did not prevent the witness from giving his opinion on the handwriting sample requested by the defence.

In a criminal case this rule does not apply in respect of witnesses who have been called by the prosecution, since they cannot be called by the defence: *R v Kelly* (1985).

A judge has a discretion to call a relevant witness in a criminal case if the prosecution fails to do so (*R v Oliva* (1965)) but the judge can only call a witness in a civil case with the agreement of the parties: *Re Enoch & Zaretsky Bock & Cos Arbitration* (1910).

A party must ensure that all their witnesses are called before the end of their case, as it is not usually possible to call a witness after the ending of a party's case: *R v Day* (1940). The judge does have a discretion, however, to permit a witness to be called if the need for the witness could not have been foreseen or anticipated earlier: *R v Scott* (1984). This is termed matters arising *ex improviso*: *R v Frost* (1839).

It is also possible to call witnesses where their evidence has only just come to light, although this is a discretion the judge will rarely exercise. In *R v Doran* (1972) the judge allowed two witnesses to be called who were members of the public in court, who had realised they had material evidence as the case was being heard.

If a party has omitted evidence by a mistake then it can usually only be admitted, at the discretion of the judge, if it is technical and uncontroversial (*Palastanga v Solman* (1962), which concerned the production of a statutory instrument). However, very exceptionally the judge will allow the calling of material evidence omitted by mistake if there is no injustice to the defence: *R v Bowles* (1992).

The course of testimony

It is normally a requirement that testimony be given in open court from the witness box.

The defendant

A defendant used to be able to make an unsworn statement from the dock in criminal cases, but this was abolished in 1982, and so the defendant should testify from the witness box. He should not testify from the dock, as this is prejudicial.

Other witnesses

Occasionally, a witness may not be able to testify from the witness box because they are scared and intimidated. This used to be of concern where children were required to testify, as their presence in court could often be traumatic and unnerving for them.

Statutory reforms have ensured that, with certain categories of child witness, this trauma can be avoided by the use of video interviews and live TV Links.

Video interviews

Section 32A Criminal Justice Act 1988, inserted by s 54 CJA 1991, allows the use in court of a video recording of an interview between an adult and a child. This pre-recorded video is played in court and operates as the child's examination in chief, thus sparing the child the ordeal of recounting their evidence in open court.

Leave is required from the trial judge, but this should be given unless the child is unavailable for cross-examination, or if the requisite notice and procedural rules have not been complied with.

Video recording is an option where the child is a witness, but not a defendant, to offences involving assault, injury or threats of injury to a person, certain cruelty offences involving children under 16, certain sexual offences, and aiding, abetting, attempting, etc of these offences. This option is only available if trial is on indictment or in the Youth Court. It is not available where trial is in the magistrates' court.

The video then stands as the child's examination in chief on any matter adequately dealt with in the video. It is still possible to examine the child in chief on matters not adequately dealt with in the video.

Live TV link

Use of live TV link is also possible whereby a child witness or, for some offences, an adult witness who is outside the UK can testify without being physically present in court. The witness is still liable to cross-examination through the TV link, but is spared the ordeal or, in some cases, inconvenience, of testifying in the court room: s 32(1) and 32(2) Criminal Justice Act 1988.

Screens

Another option is to erect a screen preventing the witness from seeing the accused. This is at the judge's discretion, and care must be taken not to unduly prejudice the defendant: *R v XYZ* (1989).

Limits on examination in chief

All questions must be relevant questions, and should usually be asked without leading the witness. A leading question is one that presupposes facts not yet in evidence, or suggests the answer to the witness. The purpose of the examination in chief is for the witness to tell his or her own story, and therefore counsel should not put words into the ness' mouth by suggesting what may or may not have happened. is possible to ask leading questions in relation to preliminary matters, or matters not in dispute, or by agreement with an opponent. Leave can also be obtained to ask leading questions of a witness who is hostile.

In the course of a trial only 'relevant' evidence (ie logically probative or disprobative) is admissible. In *DPP v Kilbourne*, this was defined as 'evidence which makes the matter which requires proof more or less probable'.

In order to be admissible it is necessary to demonstrate that the evidence or line of questioning has probative value, either directly or circumstantially, in relation to the facts in issue. This very basic fact is often overlooked, as in *R v Sandhu* (1997), a case of strict liability in criminal law where the prosecution followed the common, but incorrect, practice of using evidence to show the defendant's state of mind. Whilst this might be relevant when it came to sentencing, this was irrelevant when the issue before the court was whether the defendant was guilty. The Court of Appeal quashed the convictions.

The hostile witness

It is usual to obtain a signed proof of evidence, or witness statement prior to calling a person as a witness. This enables a party to assess what evidence a witness is capable of giving, and to prepare an effective examination in chief. Occasionally a witness will not come up to proof, ie will not repeat the story as he or she had told it in the past. This can occur for a number of reasons: the witness may be nervous, and need reassuring, or they may have forgotten details of what occurred, in which case they may be allowed to refresh their memory. It is also possible that they remember additional details, or vary their story somewhat.

Very rarely a witness will appear to be deliberately obstructive, telling a completely different story, or claiming to have completely forgotten events, or remaining silent and refusing to answer questions. Such a witness can be damaging to a party's case, and may be declared hostile. Applying to have a witness declared hostile is not a step that should be taken routinely. It may be better to try to call other witnesses to prove the point instead: *Ewer v Ambrose* (1825). In *R v Maw* (1994) it was suggested that the first step should be to invite the witness to refresh their memory by looking at their earlier statement. If the witness then persisted in being unhelpful, this might be evidence of hostility and, if the witness is an important witness, it may be necessary to apply to the judge to have them declared hostile.

It will be necessary to try to demonstrate that the witness is not merely unfavourable, but possesses a hostile *animus* towards the party calling them. This deliberate blocking of the emergence of the truth does not always come from malice; the witness may have been bribed or intimidated or trying to protect someone. By showing the judge the previous statement of the witness, the judge may be able to form an opinion on whether the witness is being deliberately obstructive or misleading or making inconsistent statements. It is not possible to introduce allegations of bad character on the part of your own witness, but once a witness is declared hostile, leading questions may be asked, to try to contradict the witness, and evidence may be given of previous inconsistent statements by the witness.

The effect of the previous inconsistent statement in criminal cases is to damage the credibility of the witness. It is not possible to take the previous statement as evidence of the truth of its contents: *R v Golder, Jones and Porritt* (1960). However, in civil cases, s 6(5) Civil Evidence Act 1995 does allow the previous inconsistent statement to be taken as proving the matters contained in it (this was also the position under s 3 Civil Evidence Act 1968).

The forgetful witness

Testifying should not be dependent upon memory; given the lapse in time between incidents and trials, it would be wrong to insist on witnesses testifying from memory. Therefore it is common practice to ask the judge for leave to allow a witness to refresh their memory from a document in the course of testifying from the witness box. It is common practice to show witnesses their statements outside the court room, and this is unobjectionable: *R v Richardson* (1971). However, many witnesses will need further assistance in court if they are to give accurate and reliable evidence. The judge will allow witnesses to refer to memory refreshing documents in order to answer questions in the witness box, although witnesses should not merely read out the contents of the document.

A memory refreshing document has two qualities. It must have been made or verified by the witness, and the witness must have done so contemporaneously to the events they were describing. Any method of recording information can be a document; it can be a written statement, a scribbled note or sketch.

A document is verified if the witness checked that another person has made a document, and that the document is accurate. This verification can be by sight or sound, as in *R v Kelsey* (1981) where a witness dictated a note to a police officer who then read it back in the presence of the witness who agreed it was correct, although the witness did not actually read the note. This should be contrasted with the case of *R v Eleftheriou* (1993) where a witness called out his observations to a colleague who noted this down. The witness did not read what had been written, nor was it read back to him, and therefore the document was not verified, and could not be used in court.

Contemporaneous documents are those that are made as soon as practicable after the event, or which are made whilst matters are still fresh in the mind of the witness. This will not be an exact period of time, but will vary from case to case, depending upon the individual facts (*R v Richardson* (1971) where the court talked of the need for 'a measure of elasticity and should not ... confine witnesses to an overly short period').

It is common for police officers to refer to notes whilst testifying. If their original notes have been used by them later to make a more detailed statement, then the more detailed statement can also be used as a memory refreshing document (*Attorney General Reference No 3 (1979)*), even if the original notes have been lost (*R v Cheng* (1976)), provided the policeman confirms that the detailed statement was made from contemporaneous notes. This might be refused if it could be argued that the detailed statement bears no resemblance to the original notes.

The memory refreshing document, and any notes it was compiled from, must be made available to the other party, who can then cross-examine the witness. However, the memory refreshing document is not usually evidence in the case and is not shown to the jury, only the witness' testimony is evidence. However, the memory refreshing document does become evidence if the opponent cross-examines by referring to a part of the document that was not used to refresh the witness' memory (*Senat v Senat* (1965)) or if the authenticity of the document is disputed: *R v Bass* (1953). Then the document will be shown to the jury. The evidential effect will then depend upon whether it is a civil or criminal trial. In criminal cases the document affects the credibility of the witness (*R v Virgo* (1978)); it cannot be used as proof of the matters it refers to. In a civil case however, the document can be used to prove the matters stated therein: s 6(5) CEA 1995.

Previous consistent statements

At common law previous consistent statements by a witness cannot be referred to. This is to prevent a witness from improving the quality of his evidence by repeating his assertions on numerous occasions. The likelihood of truth does not increase with the number of repetitions of a statement, and such statements are technically hearsay as to the truth of their contents. This suspicion of previous consistent statements is because of their self-serving nature (*R v Roberts* (1942), where the defendant's statement to his father that the shooting was accidental was held to be inadmissible because the statement was self-serving and unreliable).

Exceptions

1 Civil cases
It is possible to obtain leave from the trial judge to introduce a previous consistent statement of a witness (s 6(1) and (2) CEA 1995) and the effect of such a statement is that it can be taken as proof of the truth of its contents (s 6(5) CEA 1995).

The weight given to such statements will vary according to the circumstances of the case, and some will carry greater weight than others.

2 Memory refreshing documents
As indicated earlier, such documents are not usually evidence in the case, but if they become evidence, then they will be admissible even though they are consistent with the witness' testimony.

3 *Res gestae* statements
A witness may refer to previous consistent statements that fall within the *res gestae*, ie that are so bound up with the event to which they relate that they can be safely admitted. Such statements are explored in the chapter on common law exceptions to the rule against hearsay.

4 Statements on accusation
When a defendant is accused of a crime his reaction may be consistent with his testimony at trial. If the statement on accusation is totally exculpatory, then it is admissible to show his reaction (*R v Storey* (1968)), but it is not admissible to show the truth of its contents because it is totally self-serving.

If however, the defendant reacts by making a statement that is partly incriminatory and partly exculpatory, then the whole remark is admissible. The incriminatory remark is adverse to the maker and, as a confession, it is likely to be true. In the interests of fairness, if the prosecution use this statement the jury must be told of the defendant's complete statement, and that whilst 'the incriminatory parts are likely to be true ... the excuses do not have the same weight': *R v Duncan* (1981). The excuses will carry greater weight if made spontaneously and shortly after accusation. The greater the degree of thought or passage of time, the less weight they will attract. In *R v Aziz* (1995) the House of Lords pointed out that if the prosecution does not use the mixed statement by the defendant, then the exculpatory remarks will be inadmissible self-serving statements if tendered by the defence as evidence of their excuse or explanation.

5 Previous identifications

It is in the interests of justice to encourage and admit evidence of earlier identifications of the defendant by the witness. Although such evidence is a previous consistent statement, it will be admissible, according to *R v Christie* (1914), to show that the witness 'was able to identify at the time and to exclude the idea that the identification of the prisoner in the dock was an afterthought or mistake'. The evidence of this identification is admissible even though the witness may not be able to remember if they identified the defendant, as in *R v Osborne, R v Virtue* (1973) where a policeman testified about the prior identification of the defendant by two witnesses who had no recollection of that prior identification.

6 Rebuttal of allegation of recent fabrication

In cross-examining a witness counsel might suggest that the witness has fabricated their story at a particular point in time. It would then be possible for the party who originally called the witness to introduce evidence of a previous statement made by the witness *before* the time that they allegedly made up their story.

The allegation must be one of fabrication; it is not enough that an accusation of lying has been made: *Fox v General Medical Council* (1960). A lie cannot be disproved by pointing to an earlier repetition of the same story. However if the allegation is that, for example, the witness made up the story on Friday, this can be disproved by showing that the witness was saying the same thing the previous Monday. This occurred in *R v Oyesiku* (1971) where a witness was accused in cross-examination of making up her story after she had conversed with her husband in jail. Evidence was then admitted of a previous consistent statement made by the witness to her solicitor *before* she had had the opportunity to speak to her husband.

7 Recent complaints in sexual offences

This exception is viewed by many as anachronistic (the Law Commission has suggested its abolition in its report on hearsay evidence). However, at present it is possible to introduce evidence of a previous consistent statement made by a male or female victim of a wide range of sexual offences: *R v Camelleri* (1922). The victim must testify in order for the previous complaint to be admissible. In *R v Wallwork* (1958) a child's complaint was inadmissible as the child herself was too young to testify, and therefore it was purely hearsay.

To be admissible the complaint must be made as soon as practicable after the alleged offence, and this is not a strict time limit, but will vary with the circumstances of the case: *R v Cummings* (1948). Consideration will be given to how traumatised the victim was, how badly injured they were, who was available for them to talk to, etc.

In *R v Valentine* (1996) the court acknowledged that it was often difficult for victims of sexual offences to bring themselves to mention their ordeal to others. For this reason it was important not to place too strict a time limit on what would amount to a complaint made as soon as practicable.

The complaint must also be voluntary, ie a complaint that the witness wanted to make, not one that was forced out of them: *R v Osborne* (1905). A complaint made in response to a question will still be admissible provided the questioning was not leading or inducing or intimidating.

The evidential effect of such a previous consistent statement was explained in *R v Lillyman* (1896), as reinforcing the consistency and credibility of the witness, and if consent was an issue in the case, such a complaint could support lack of consent.

Use of document: the 'best evidence' rule

The 'best evidence' rule developed at common law to ensure the accuracy of the contents of documentary evidence. The original document needed to be used, and secondary evidence by way of a copy or oral evidence from someone who had seen the document was inadmissible to prove what the document contained: *Augustien v Challis* (1847). However, secondary evidence was admissible to prove the existence of the document: *R v Elworthy* (1867). This best evidence rule does not apply to modern forms of documents, such as films (*Kajala v Noble* (1982)), and many statutes now provide for the use of original documents or a copy (Criminal Justice Act 1988; Civil Evidence Act 1995).

4 Cross-examination

Introduction

Once a witness has taken the oath they can be cross-examined by the opposing party, even if the witness has given no examination in chief. If there is no opportunity to cross-examine, because, for example, the witness has died or is too distressed to continue the examination in chief, the evidence is still admissible but will carry no weight: *R v Stretton* (1988). In extreme cases if the injustice is too great, the trial will need to be abandoned: *R v Lawless* (1994).

A failure to cross-examine will be taken as acceptance of the witness' evidence (*R v Fenlon* (1980)), and it is counsel's duty to make it clear to the witness which aspect of the evidence is not accepted.

The Bar Code of Conduct

Counsel's duty is to challenge any part of the witness' evidence that runs contrary to his instructions, to put any allegation to the witness that would be proper in the conduct of the defence, and to put to the witness any aspect of counsel's case that the witness may be able to assist with.

Counsel should be fearless in his cross-examination but should avoid being unnecessarily or gratuitously offensive, and avoid unnecessary time wasting. Only counsel can cross-examine the child witness or victim of certain offences, s 55(7) Criminal Justice Act 1991.

The aim of cross-examination

Cross-examination is designed to serve one or more of the following purposes:
- to damage or destroy the opponent's case;
- to substantially discredit the witness;
- to support one's own case.

Relevance and admissibility of cross-examination

All cross-examination must be relevant and, if evidence is inadmissible in chief, it is usually inadmissible in cross-examination (*R v Treacy* (1944) which was a case involving a confession that was ruled inadmissible for the prosecution).

However, if the confession of D1 is ruled inadmissible for the prosecution, but contains material that could assist a co-accused D2, then D2's counsel can cross-examine D1 on the otherwise inadmissible confession as it has a relevance to D2's defence: *R v Rowson* (1986). However, the jury must be told that, whilst the confession may be evidence for D2, it is not evidence against D1.

This rule does not operate in reverse, however. If D1 makes a confession in which he incriminates himself and D2, this is admissible evidence against D1, not D2. Consequently, D1 can be cross-examined about the statement, but D2 cannot as it is inadmissible against him *R v Windass* (1989).

The only possible way round this would be to show the statement to D2, ask him to read it and ask if he agrees that it is true. If he is foolish enough to accept the statement he can be cross-examined on it: *R v Cross* (1990).

Discrediting witnesses

It is a proper function of cross-examination to seek to substantially discredit the witness in appropriate cases: *Hobbs v Tinling* (1929). It is not a correct use of cross-examination if the incidents are so trivial or remote in time that they can have little or no bearing on the witness' credibility.

Consequently, ordinary witnesses can be asked about their bad character and previous convictions if this would seriously discredit them.

The complainant in rape cases

Whilst witness can usually be asked about matters that substantially discredit them, special rules apply to complainants in sexual offences being asked about their previous sexual experience. There was in the past a regrettable tendency to routinely explore details of the complainant's private sexual experience, often with the result that such complainants felt it was they, and not the accused, that was on trial. This deterred many complainants from coming forward, and the law was reformed by s 2 Sexual Offences (Amendment) Act 1976.

The restriction in s 2 Sexual Offences (Amendment) Act 1976

This Act applies to the cross-examination of complainants (both male and female) in rape offences. This includes rape, attempted rape and burglary with intent to rape, and any form of aiding, abetting, counselling, procuring, inciting or conspiring such offences. All other sexual offences are governed by the common law, although in *R v Funderburk* (1990) the Court of Appeal indicated that the common law would adopt a similar policy to that in s 2.

Section 2 prohibits the asking of questions of the complainant about her sexual experience with men *other than* the defendant unless leave is obtained from the trial judge.

This does not prevent cross-examination on her sexual experience *with* the defendant, and this is always likely to be highly relevant: *R v Riley* (1887). However, it is clear that her sexual experience with other men is less likely to be relevant, and may just gratuitously embarrass and humiliate the complainant.

'Sexual experience' covers a wide range of sexual activity and is not limited to sexual intercourse. Talking about sexual activity may be included (*R v Hinds* (1979)), outrageous flirting (*R v Viola* (1992)) as well as physical intimacy with others. However, the restriction applies only to sexual experience with persons other than the accused. The restriction does not prevent cross-examination about sexual experience that does not involve others, for example, with animals or sex toys, provided it is relevant, as in *R v Barnes* (1994) where the complainant was asked about the use of a vibrator.

When will leave be granted

Section 2 requires that the judge should only give leave if he is satisfied 'that it would be unfair to the defendant to refuse to allow the evidence to be adduced or the question to be asked'.

This question of unfairness was considered in *R v Lawrence* (1977) where it was stated that the trial judge 'must take the view that it is more likely than not that the particular question ... might reasonably lead the jury, properly directed in the summing up, to take a different view of the complainant's evidence from that which they might take if the question ... was ... not allowed'.

This test of causing the jury to take a different view was approved in *R v Mills* (1978) where it was quite clear that cross-examination whose sole purpose is to gratuitously blacken the complainant's character by reference to her sexual experience should not be allowed. If, however, her sexual experience is of relevance to the issues, it can rightly be explored in cross-examination (*R v C* (1996)), and the correct test is relevance to the issues, not the quality of the evidence supporting the application.

Circumstances where there may be unfairness to the accused

The following are circumstances where case law has shown possible unfairness to the accused. Remember, each case depends on its individual facts, and that, since this is a matter of judicial discretion, some judges may be more willing to permit cross-examination than others.

* Extreme promiscuity

  It seems that if a woman or man has been extremely promiscuous in the past, then this can be explored in cross-examination: *R v Bashir* (1969). This may be relevant in that it could mean that the complainant was more likely to consent to sex with someone she had only just met.

- False allegations of rape
  If the complainant has made false allegations of rape in the past, then this can properly be raised in cross-examination (*R v Cox* (1987)) as this may tend to show that the complainant consented but regretted it later, or that she is substantially discreditable.
- Sexual experience close in time
  In *R v Viola* (1982) the complainant alleged rape and leave was sought to cross-examine her about the sexual experience involving others just before and after the alleged rape. This should have been allowed as the behaviour before and after the rape was so close in time that it tended to suggest that the complainant had been a willing participant in sexual intercourse, not rape.
- Knowledge of sexual experience and belief in consent
  Whilst it will not be open to a defendant to routinely cross-examine a complainant about her sexual experience because he argues that such experience led him to believe she was consenting, there are some circumstances where it would be unfair to prohibit the cross-examination: *R v Barton* (1986). It is submitted that mere knowledge that a woman has had sexual experience with another cannot justify cross-examination but if the previous sexual experience was known to have arisen in very similar factual circumstances to those the defendant found himself in, then cross-examination may be justified.
- To rebut the impression given by the complainant in examination in chief
  Sometimes the complainant testifies and, to support her allegations of lack of consent, says something which seems consistent with the intercourse being non-consensual. This may then open the way for cross-examination about previous sexual experience if this would show that what the complainant said was untrue, and that what she says is as consistent with consensual intercourse as it is with rape.
  In *R v Riley* (1991) the complainant alleged rape, and stated that she had not consented, since she would never voluntarily have sex when her child was asleep in the same room. This opened the way for cross-examination about a previous sexual experience with another man in which the complainant had agreed to intercourse even though the child was sleeping in the room. This tended to show the complainant was lying and also that the presence of the child was as consistent with consensual as it was with non-consensual intercourse.
  Likewise in *R v Ellis* (1990) the complainant alleged rape and stated that she felt dirty and degraded and had to keep bathing. Evidence

was admissible about previous consensual intercourse with another man, after which the complainant had told her friend she felt dirty and degraded.

- Sadistic circumstances

  A rather bizarre example is the case of *R v SMS* (1992) in which the defendant was accused of raping a 14 year old girl in particularly sordid and revolting circumstances. His defence was consent, and the Court of Appeal held that cross-examination of the complainant should have been allowed to the extent of establishing whether she was a virgin or had some sexual experience at the time. The jury would have been left with the impression that she was a virgin and would have found it hard to believe that she would consent to intercourse in the circumstances of the case. Apparently the Court of Appeal thought that if the jury had known she was sexually experienced they may have taken a different view of the evidence!

The common law position: *R v Funderburk*

In *R v Funderburk* the defendant was accused of unlawful intercourse with a young girl. The effect of her evidence was to suggest that she had lost her virginity to the defendant. The defendant denied that any intercourse had taken place, and wished to cross-examine the girl about previous sexual experience with other men. The Court of Appeal held that leave should have been granted to allow the question, the common law adopting a similar approach to such cross-examination as s 2. The cross-examination would not have gratuitously blackened the complainant's character. Instead, if the jury had known that she had sexual intercourse with another man, they would have taken a different view of the evidence. The sex that she described and attributed to the defendant was capable of being a transposing of her experience with the other man. This could support the defence that the intercourse did not take place with the defendant, but in fact occurred with another man.

Previous inconsistent statements

When a witness answers questions in cross-examination, cross-examining counsel must decide what to do when faced with an answer that does not accord with his case. Counsel is not obliged to accept that the witness is telling the truth, and can assert that the answer is a lie, or the witness mistaken. However, the extent to which it is possible to contradict the witness' answer by calling rebutting evidence depends upon whether the question related to the facts in issue or was relevant only to a collateral issue.

Rebutting answers to questions relevant to the subject-matter of the dispute

If the question is relevant to the subject-matter of the dispute then rebutting evidence may be called; this includes the use of previous inconsistent statements. The appropriate provisions are to be found in ss 4 and 5 Criminal Procedure Act 1865 which applies to both civil and criminal trials.

Section 4 Criminal Procedure Act 1865

Section 4 applies to both oral and written inconsistent statements. It provides that if the witness is asked about a previous inconsistent statement that is relevant to the subject-matter of the dispute, and the witness does not distinctly admit that he made the statement, then proof can be given that he made the statement.

Whether a statement is relevant to the subject-matter of the dispute or is merely collateral can be a difficult distinction to make in sexual cases. In *R v Funderburk* the Court of Appeal thought that in sexual cases where it is often one person's word against the other as to what occurred, the distinction is virtually non-existent. By destroying credibility it will tend to spill over into subject-matter, and to suggest that the offence never took place as alleged. In *Funderburk* itself the question about previous sexual experience went to the subject-matter of the dispute. So, when the complainant denied telling her friend about her previous sexual experience, the inconsistent statement could be proved by calling the friend under s 4 CPA 1865.

Section 4 allows the cross-examiner to prove the inconsistent statement if it is not distinctly admitted. Therefore, proof is possible if the witness is evasive, not just where he absolutely denies the statement. However, before proof is possible the witness must be reminded of the statement and given the opportunity to acknowledge he made it.

Section 5 Criminal Procedures Act 1865

This applies to written statements only and, as in s 4, this must be relevant to the subject-matter of the proceedings. Under s 5 cross-examination is possible without showing the witness the written statement, thus keeping an element of surprise or disadvantage.

If the witness still persists in not admitting the statement then the cross-examiner could leave matters where they stand, or could go on to prove the inconsistent statement. At this point the written statement must be shown to the witness in order for the inconsistent statement to be proved. Counsel must always have the document in court, even if it is not proposed to contradict the witness: *R v Anderson* (1929).

By proving the inconsistent statement the document becomes evidence, and there is the risk that it may contain material that is helpful to the opponent as well as damaging material. The judge may allow the jury to see the whole document, but there is a discretion to restrict the inspection to those parts of the document that were used in cross-examination.

Effect of previous inconsistent statement

Criminal cases

In a criminal case, the previous inconsistent statement goes to the witness' credibility. It is not capable of proving the truth of the subject-matter of its contents: *R v Askey* (1981).

Civil cases

In civil cases, the Civil Evidence Act 1995 preserves the rules regarding previous inconsistent statements: s 6(3). However, the effect of the statement goes beyond the credibility of the witness and can be proof of the truth of its contents: s 6(5).

Finality of answers to collateral issues

The general rule is that if a witness is asked a question that is not relevant to a fact in issue, but merely relates to a collateral issue, then the witness' answer must be accepted as final. This does not mean that counsel has to accept the answer as correct, rather it means that no evidence in rebuttal will be permitted, either by calling witnesses or proving inconsistent statements.

What is collateral?

In *AG v Hitchcock* (1847) a collateral issue was described as one 'when the question is not relevant, strictly speaking, to the issue, but tending to contradict the witness'. In this case a witness giving evidence about the workings of a water cistern was asked in cross-examination whether he had been offered a bribe. The witness denied this and counsel was not permitted to call rebutting evidence. The offering of a bribe to the witness was not directly relevant to the workings of the cistern, but went to a side issue. There must be a limit to the exploration of side issues since this would be time consuming and confusing. The rule on finality avoids never-ending collateral disputes, as was explained in *AG v Hitchcock*:

The question why a party is obliged to take the answer of the witness is that if he was permitted to go into it, it is only justice to allow the witness to call evidence in support of the evidence he has just given, and as those witnesses might be cross-examined as to their conduct, such a course would be productive of endless collateral issues.

Consequently, collateral issues tend to relate to the credibility of the witness or other issues that arise in the trial but can be regarded as side issues.

Exceptions to the rule on finality

1 Previous convictions
Since it is a legitimate purpose of cross-examination to seek to substantially discredit a witness (*Hobbs v Tinling* (1929)), it is permissible to ask a witness whether they have previous convictions. If they answer incorrectly then s 6 Criminal Procedure Act 1865 allows proof to be given of the previous convictions.

2 Bias or partiality
Very few witnesses are truly independent. Most know one or other of the parties or have reason to favour one side. This does not necessarily amount to bias in the sense required as an exception to the rule on finality.

If a witness purports to be an independent witness, but is in reality concealing the true nature of their relationship with one of the parties, then they can be asked about the relationship and, if they deny it, the relationship can be proved as it exhibits possibly an attempt to mislead the jury, see *Thomas v David* (1836), where the witness denied being the plaintiff's mistress and rebutting evidence was allowed.

Bias or partiality may also exist if it can be argued that the witness is prepared to go to any lengths to cheat and deceive the jury. In *R v Mendy* (1976) the defendant's husband had been seen talking to one of the witnesses as they emerged after giving their evidence in court. He was asked about this in cross-examination and he denied it. Rebutting evidence was permitted. This was one easily proven incident and was not productive of never-ending collateral issues.

In *R v Busby* (1984) a police officer was cross-examined as to whether he had threatened defence witnesses. The policeman denied this, and evidence was admitted to rebut his answer. Again this was an easily proven incident. Contrast this with *R v Edwards* (1991) where the defence sought to cross-examine a police officer about alleged fabricated evidence in earlier trials. Allegations of fabrication would substantially discredit the witness, and the court thought that it was right to allow cross-examination about previous trials that had resulted in acquittals where it could be inferred that the jury disbelieved the police officer's evidence. It would not be right to cross-examine about unadjudicated cases or complaints about the police officer. The police officer concerned then denied fabrication in earlier trials, and the defence sought to admit evidence about the earlier trials. This was held to be inadmissible. What went on at the earlier trials was clearly a collateral issue, relating to the witness' credibility. The rule on finality prevented the calling of such rebutting evidence, since it would be productive of too many collateral issues and be difficult to prove, time consuming and confuse the real issues at the defendant's trial.

3 Reputation for untruthfulness

It is possible to suggest in cross-examination that a witness has a bad reputation for being untruthful. If the witness denies this then rebutting evidence may be called in the form of a person who knows the witness. That person can give evidence of the witness' general reputation for untruthfulness but not the reasons why the witness is regarded as untruthful: *R v Richardson* (1969).

4 Medical evidence of unreliability

If a witness suffers from some abnormality of mind or disorder that affects the reliability of his evidence then it may be suggested by his cross-examiner that he is incapable of telling the truth. If he denies it, then rebutting evidence in the form of expert opinion evidence is admissible.

In *Toohey v MPC* (1965) the victim accused the defendant of robbery, but the evidence pointed to the victim suffering hysteria which affected the reliability of his evidence. Medical evidence was admissible from a doctor who had examined the victim as to the nature and extent of his condition and how it would affect his reliability.

5 Impeaching admissible hearsay

If hearsay is admissible under the Civil Evidence Act 1995 or the Criminal Justice Act 1988, then it is possible to attack the credibility of the maker of the hearsay statement.

Re-examination

Once cross-examination of the witness ends he may be re-examined by the party calling him. Re-examination deals with issues not raised in cross-examination and attempts to repair any damage done. Leading questions are not permissible.

5 Similar fact evidence

Introduction

When a defendant is on trial charged with an offence, the general rule is that he should be tried for his behaviour in the count on the indictment, and that no mention should be made of his bad or discreditable behaviour on other occasions. It follows from this that, when a defendant is tried for a number of offences, the evidence on each offence should be considered separately, without taking into account what is alleged in the other counts.

To bring such behaviour to the jury's attention is usually highly prejudicial, and in most cases the past behaviour of the defendant is of little or no logical relevance to his guilt of the offence for which he is on trial. The fact that he has behaved in a particular way in the past is no guarantee that he has behaved in the same way again, nor does it mean that he is more likely to commit the offence than the next man. The past tendency towards criminal activity cannot, therefore, be used by the prosecution to show that the defendant is more likely to be guilty of the present offence, or else it would be a classic case of giving a dog a bad name and hanging him.

There are however, certain cases where the past behaviour cannot be ignored, as it is highly relevant to the issues before the jury. Such extremely relevant evidence is labelled 'similar fact evidence' although like all labels this can be misleading. It is important to remember that it is not enough for there to be a similarity between the facts of the cases. It must be demonstrated that there is such a high degree of relevance, what is called 'positive probative value', that the evidence should be admitted, notwithstanding that it may be prejudicial to the defendant.

The search for positive probative value

In *Makin v AG of New South Wales* (1894) the defendants were on trial for murdering a young child whose body had been found buried in the garden of a house once occupied by the defendants. The defendants had agreed to take the child into their care, on receipt of a sum of money from the mother. This money was insufficient to pay for the child's long-term upkeep and, from the evidence afforded by the child's body, it had met with its death shortly after being left in the defendants' care by the mother. The prosecution was contending that the child had been deliberately killed by the defendants, rather than dying through natural causes, and just being wrongly buried without notifying the authorities. In support of this, the prosecution tendered evidence that 13 other dead children had been found buried in various gardens of properties occupied by the defendants, all of whom had been taken in from their mothers for care by the defendants in return for small payments. This evidence was admissible since it did more than just show previous bad behaviour or character. It was relevant to the issue before the jury, ie was the death deliberate and the responsibility of the defendants. To have found other bodies in such strikingly similar circumstances was inexplicable on the basis of coincidence, and enormously probative of the defendants' guilt.

Makin was used subsequently to justify admitting evidence on the basis of a striking similarity between the facts of the offence with which the defendant was charged, and the previous behaviour. This led the courts to often strain the meaning of the phrase striking similarity, and care should be exercised when dealing with older cases on the meaning of striking similarity. The modern view is that the correct test of admissibility is whether the evidence of the defendant's behaviour on other occasions is relevant to an issue before the jury, and is 'positively probative': *R v Lunt* (1987). It is not always necessary for the positive probative value to exhibit striking similarity.

This was the conclusion of the House of Lords in the landmark decision of *R v P* (1991) (or *DPP v P* (1991)). In this case a father was accused of sexually abusing his two young daughters. Both girls claimed to have been raped and abused by their father, with their mother apparently knowing, or turning a blind eye to, what was happening. The father behaved in a very domineering manner to both girls, was an extreme disciplinarian and had paid for both girls to have abortions. Normally the evidence of each girl would have been considered separately, but if their evidence could be regarded as similar fact evidence in relation to one another then what one girl said could be used to support the case against the father in relation to the other girl, and *vice versa*. There was a great deal in common between the two accounts of the girls, but the features were the sort of features that would be commonly encountered in allegations of sexual abuse by fathers to their daughters. The evidence certainly did not exhibit 'striking similarity' as there was little that was unusual, given the fact that sexual abuse of children is now acknowledged to be more widespread than used to be thought. However, the House of Lords held that it was enough that the girls' accounts revealed a strong underlying link, in that the evidence of what happened to one girl was positively probative in relation to the other allegation. There was no doubt as to the identity of the offender, the only question was whether the abuse was actually taking place. In such circumstances, the positive probative value did not need to come from striking similarity, something less would suffice. However, if identity is in issue then the House of Lords thought that it would still be necessary to seek striking similarity, ie the repetition of a feature or features that was sufficiently unusual to amount to a signature or hallmark.

In *R v West* the defendant, Rose West, was on trial for 10 murders, and she ran a defence that they were all the responsibility of her husband, who had killed himself before the trial. The prosecution were allowed to use the similarity between seven of the murders to show that it was likely that the same person (or persons) was responsible for the deaths of these victims. All seven victims had been found buried in and under a home occupied by the defendant and her husband, all were buried naked, tied up and mutilated. The prosecution case was that the defendant had participated in the killings as part of her perverted sexual gratification in acts of sadistic sexual violence. Evidence was admitted from four victims of sadistic sexual assaults by the defendant, as this had positive probative value in showing that she had been involved in the killings, and that it was unlikely that they could have occurred without her knowledge.

Identity cases and the search for striking similarity

Where the prosecution seeks to identify the defendant as the person responsible for a crime by reference to his other discreditable behaviour, then that behaviour must exhibit positive probative value in the form of striking similarity. There will need to be such enormous probative value in the past behaviour that it is safe to admit it to identify the defendant, as opposed to anyone else, as being responsible for the crime in question. Whether there is striking similarity will depend on the facts of the case, and it is important to analyse the similarities and differences between the crimes: *R v Johnson* (1995).

In *Boardman v DPP* (1975) the House of Lords gave guidance on what might properly be regarded as striking similarity. *Boardman* was a case where a number of boys were making allegations of indecent assault against the defendant, who was the headmaster at their boarding school. The boys said they had been woken at night and lured to the headmaster's room where they had been encouraged to play the active role in the buggery. The ordinary approach would be to consider the evidence in relation to the offences against each boy separately but if the evidence amounted to similar fact evidence then the evidence on the counts would be cross admissible, ie what Boy A said could be admitted to support what Boy B said, and *vice versa*. (Many of these early cases involve the issues of similar fact evidence and corroboration, although the latter is no longer a consideration since the Criminal Justice and Public Order Act 1994.)

The House of Lords considered the evidence and held that it was similar fact evidence, a result that would still be correct applying the positive probative value test of *R v P* or *DPP v P*. There was clearly a very strong underlying link between what each boy said, and the fact that more than one boy was making such allegations did tend to suggest that the offences may have been more likely than not to have taken place. *Boardman* was not a case in which the defence was arguing mistaken identity; they were disputing that the offences ever took the Criminal Proceedings and Investigations Act 1996 is fully in force the defence will be required to give an outline of their defence in advance of the trial, and the significance of past behaviour will be easier to determine.

Multiple accusations

Where a defendant is on trial accused of similar offences by a number of different victims it may be possible to admit the evidence of what one victim says to support the account of the other, and *vice versa*. Such cross admissibility can be justified on the basis that the allegations have a strong underlying link, and the fact that more than one person is accusing the defendant of such behaviour has positive probative value, in suggesting that the incidents did occur, and there is accordingly similar fact evidence. In such cases the identity of the offender is not an issue; what needs to be determined is whether the offences ever took place as alleged by the victims.

In *Boardman v DPP* (1975) the allegations by the boys against the headmaster all bore a strong underlying link, and there were a number of common features in their accounts. The fact that they all made such very similar allegations against the defendant justified cross admissibility, since it was unlikely that they would all make up such stories.

When considering whether there is positive probative value it is necessary for the judge to assume that the victims are telling the truth, and ignore the possibility that they have colluded to fabricate or falsify their accounts: *R v H* (1994). In this case the House of Lords had to consider a number of allegations of sexual abuse by the defendant against victims who had talked to each other and had the opportunity of colluding. It was held that since the nature of such multiple accusations often meant the victims were known to each other and could have influenced one another, this needed to be ignored by the judge in considering the similar fact nature of the evidence. Otherwise defendants need only to allege collusion to prevent the evidence qualifying as similar fact. As such it was not necessary to hold a *voir dire* to investigate the possibility of collusion. Instead collusion was a factor that should be raised in the presence of the jury, as it went to the weight to be given to the accounts, not to their admissibility.

R v P or *DPP v P* is another multiple accusation case where there was such a resemblance between the two girls' accounts that what each girl said could support the other girl's account, and *vice versa*.

place, and saying that the boys were making up the allegations. However, the House of Lords applied the test of striking similarity to the facts, as it was thought at that time that this was the correct interpretation of *Makin*. The features of *Boardman* were considered to be just about within striking similarity, the most unusual feature being the active role the boys were asked to play. Now it would not be necessary to try to establish striking similarity where identity was not an issue, but the House of Lords' comments on this point are useful guidance.

Lord Salmon said:

If the crime charged were committed in a uniquely or strikingly similar manner to other crimes committed by the accused ... this may be evidence on which the jury could reasonably conclude that the accused was guilty of the crime charged. The similarity would have to be so unique or striking that common sense makes it inexplicable on the basis of coincidence.

According to Lord Cross it is whether the evidence 'would point so strongly to his guilt that only the ultra cautious jury, if they accepted it as true, would acquit in the face of it'.

Famous examples of homosexual rape wearing a red Indian headdress and burglary by entering down the chimney and leaving messages in lipstick were cited.

In *R v Scarrott* (1977) the defendant was on trial accused of buggery and indecent assault against a number of young boys, and Lord Justice Scarman stated:

Positive probative value is what the law requires if similar fact evidence is to be admissible. Such probative value is not provided by the mere repetition of similar facts; there has to be some feature or features in the evidence sought to be adduced which provides a link, an underlying link as it has been called in some of the cases. The existence of such a link is not to be inferred from mere similarity of facts which are themselves so commonplace that they can provide no sure ground for saying that they point to the commission by the accused of the offence under consideration.

If the evidence does exhibit striking similarity then it will be possible to admit details of the defendant's past bad behaviour and offences. These so called signature or hallmark crimes can be seen in cases like *R v Straffen* (1952) where the defendant was on trial for the murder of a young girl, who had been killed at a time when the defendant was on the run from a prison hospital. This girl had been killed in an unusual way, and the defendant had two previous convictions for such unusual murders. These convictions were admissible.

Striking similarity may also be an issue when the defendant is on trial for a number of offences, and the prosecution case is that the offences were all the work of the one man. To establish that this is the case, the offences must exhibit a striking similarity between themselves. In *R v Mansfield* (1977) the defendant was accused of arson in three counts on an indictment. The fires all bore a striking similarity in that they had been started in unusual ways. It was therefore possible to direct the jury that the fires could be the work of the one man, and invite them to consider whether there is sufficient evidence that the defendant was that one man.

It is vital to ensure that there is evidence linking the defendant with at least one of the crimes before he can be convicted of them all. In *R v McGranaghan* (1995) the defendant had been convicted of burglaries involving rape and indecent assaults. The offences bore sufficient similarity that they could be considered the work of one man, and there was cross admissibility. However, there was only poor quality identification evidence linking the defendant to one of the crimes, and the Court of Appeal thought that the conviction was unsafe since there was insufficient evidence linking the defendant to the crimes.

A case where there was sufficient evidence linking the defendant to the crimes was *R v Black* (1995). Black was accused of a number of murders on young girls, which bore striking similarities, and could be considered the work of the one man. To link the defendant with those crimes the prosecution used, amongst other evidence, the fact that the defendant had an earlier conviction that had similar fact qualities. This conviction could safely link him to the crimes on the indictment.

If the defendant is on trial for a number of offences with similar fact qualities, it may also be possible for the jury to infer that the identification evidence of a number of witnesses can be added together to link the defendant with the crime. Since the crimes are the work of the one man, an identification by a witness to crime 1 can be added to the identification evidence of the witness to crime 2, since they are in essence both describing the same man: *R v Downey* (1995), *R v Barnes* (1995).

Positive probative value in the form of strong underlying links

Where identity is not an issue it is sufficient to establish positive probative value, in the form of evidence that is so probative in relation to an issue before the jury that it outweighs any prejudice done to the defendant by admitting the evidence.

The starting point is to consider what the issues before the jury are, and how the defendant's behaviour on other occasions has probative

value in helping to prove those issues. Remember it is not enough to show that something has happened before; there must be greater probative force than that.

In *R v Smith* (1915) the defendant was accused of murdering his wife, who had been found drowned in her bath in a bathroom with no lock on the door. The defendant had heavily insured her life, and told those investigating her death that she had probably had an epileptic fit. The defendant had also had two previous wives die in such circumstances. The issue before the jury was whether the death was a genuine accident or whether the defendant had been responsible, the motive being financial gain. The fact that the defendant had three wives die in this way made accidental death extremely unlikely. This is the kind of case where common sense indicates that the possibility of coincidence is remote, and deliberate design more likely.

Contrast this with *Noor Mohammed v R* (1949) where the defendant was accused of murdering a woman who had died from cyanide poisoning. At that time it was not uncommon for people to use small doses of what would be regarded as poison to obtain pain relief, and accidental overdose was plausible. There was some evidence of discord between the defendant and the woman, and there was also the possibility that she had committed suicide. The defendant had access to cyanide through his work as a goldsmith but, since there was no evidence of his giving the cyanide to the woman, the case against him was very weak, and the evidence of motive not as strong as *R v Smith* (1915). However, the prosecution sought to use evidence relating to the death of his wife, who had also died of cyanide poisoning. The defendant had been overheard giving her some cyanide to help with toothache. Here the cases had in common the cause of death of both women, and the sexual relationship they both had with the defendant. However the prosecution could not establish any stronger links, and therefore the evidence about the wife merely increased suspicion, and prejudiced the defendant without sufficient probative value.

Clearly probative value will depend to a great extent on the facts of the individual case and can be influenced by what defence the defendant is relying on. It is not a good idea to have a rigid view that evidence is admissible for certain defences and not for others. It is preferable to take a wider view of the case in its entirety, although judges frequently do categorise relevance by reference to the defence being relied on!

The prosecution cannot credit the defence with fanciful defences in order to admit evidence that should otherwise be inadmissible. When

Examples of positive probative value in non-identity cases

In *R v Ball* (1911) a brother and sister were accused of incest. They had lived together and had a child before incest was a crime, and they continued to live together after incest was criminalised. The prosecution needed to prove that sexual intercourse took place between them. This is not a matter where there are usually eye witnesses other than the individuals involved! Consequently the prosecution needs to rely on circumstantial evidence. The traditional test is to see whether the couple have had the opportunity to have intercourse (which they had here) and whether they had the inclination. The jury would normally find it hard to believe that a brother and sister were sexually attracted to each other, but if the evidence of the previous sexual nature of their relationship were to be admitted then this would alter the jury's view. The evidence was felt to have sufficient probative value to justify its admission, although it clearly shows a disposition to certain behaviour. This shows how important it is to take an overall view of the case rather than rely on bland assertions such as evidence of disposition is not admissible. Usually disposition towards certain behaviour is not admissible because it normally lacks probative value. In some cases, however, there will be positive probative value and admissibility will be justified. Similar fact evidence is a question of relevance and is heavily dependent on the facts of each case, and it is misleading to rely on strict categorisation of cases.

In *R v Barrington* (1981) the defendant was accused of indecently assaulting a young girl who had been lured to the house by an advert seeking a babysitter. When there she alleged she had been told the defendants were in the film and photography business, shown indecent photographs, asked to pose nude and then assaulted. The defendants denied that anything like this had occurred. The prosecution called evidence from other girls who had been lured to the premises on similar pretexts and had been treated in the same way, save for being indecently assaulted. These accounts were admissible since they had positive probative value in that they tended to show that the victim has not made up her account. The fact that she and the others told such very similar stories was 'inexplicable on the basis of coincidence' and tended to show the events had occurred. The accounts of the other girls would not have been admissible if the defendants had admitted what occurred but argued that it happened consensually. None of the other girls was forced to participate in the indecent acts, and so their accounts had no probative value if the allegation was that there was no consent.

Likewise in *R v Butler* (1987) the defendant was accused of raping a woman and forcing her to engage in oral sex as he drove along. The defendant denied being the man responsible. Evidence was admitted from the defendant's girlfriend that she willingly engaged in such activities with him at the location of the alleged rape. This was admitted as it had probative value in that it supported the victim's identification of her attacker. It would not have been admissible if the defendant had admitted being involved, but argued consent, since the activities with the girlfriend had no probative value where lack of consent was argued.

The defendant in *R v Rodley* (1913) was accused of burglary with intent to rape, and the prosecution sought to admit evidence that he had entered another house by the chimney an hour later and had consensual intercourse with the woman there. This was inadmissible as it had no relevance to whether the defendant intended rape; it merely showed a very unusual way of entering premises!

There is a grave risk of prejudice if evidence of the defendant's behaviour is admitted without careful scrutiny of its relevance. In *R v Tricoglus* (1977) the defendant was accused of murdering a prostitute, which he denied. Evidence that a man fitting the defendant's description had been seen talking to prostitutes in the area was inadmissible. It did not have probative value, in that talking to a prostitute does not tend to show the man would go on to kill another prostitute, and it is the kind of evidence where the jury would be inclined to accord it a prejudicial significance.

Sexual offences and the significance of sexual disposition

Where a defendant is charged with a sexual offence it is important not lose sight of the need for positive probative value, and striking similarity if identity is in issue. Older cases tend to reflect judicial repugnance and distaste for homosexuality and paedophilia, which would now be considered a dangerous approach to take. In *R v Thompson* (1976) the defendant was accused of homosexual offences against a number of boys who told the police that the defendant had arranged to meet them in a particular place at a later date. The police arrested the defendant who was at the appointed place at the arranged time. He was found to possess powder puffs and indecent photographs, which the House of Lords thought were items associated with homosexual tendencies. This was admissible to confirm his identity and

Lord Sumner stated that homosexuality and sexual offences involving children could be regarded as 'particular perverted lust' and therefore admissible where the defendant was charged with a homosexual offence.

This was also accepted in *R v Sims* (1946) where the homosexuality of the defendant was viewed as abnormal and perverted and therefore admissible, likewise in *R v King* (1982). However in *R v Horwood* (1970) this automatic admissibility was questioned, and the court stressed the need for the homosexuality to be relevant. In *Boardman v DPP* (1975) the House of Lords stressed that sexual cases were to be treated no differently from others, and the evidence of the defendant's sexuality needed to be positively probative in the same way as his other behaviour.

The result in *R v Thompson* is probably still correct, in that for the defendant to be found where the boys said he would be, and for him to be identified by them, and for him to have items associated with homosexuality was 'inexplicable on the basis of coincidence' and tended to suggest that he had been correctly identified.

Consequently it would seem that it is necessary to demonstrate that the defendant's sexual behaviour has a positive probative value in respect of an issue before the jury. The courts have tended in this respect to draw a distinction between identity cases, where homosexuality or paedophilia is unlikely in itself to possess the quality of striking similarity necessary to identify the defendant as opposed to any other person as being responsible, and cases where the defendant is relying on a defence of innocent association. Innocent association cases are cases where the defendant admits being with the victim but denies that any impropriety took place. Clearly there was opportunity, and it may be that the defendant's past tendencies can be used to prove his sexual inclination. This was the basis of *R v Lewis* (1982) where the defendant's interest in paedophilia was admitted as having positive probative value as to whether his contact with the children was indecent or innocent.

Possession of incriminating items

If the defendant is found in possession of items of the sort that could have been used in the crimes in question then the court will admit the evidence as having positive probative value, even though there is no proof that the items were actually used.

This can be seen in *R v Thompson* (1976) with the powder puffs, and in *R v Reading* (1966) where the defendant was accused of having been involved in robberies and lorry hijacking and was found in possession of number plates and radios which could have been used in the offences although it was not possible to show they were actually used. These items were admissible, as were stolen credit cards in the possession of a defendant accused of dishonestly using credit cards (*R v Mustafa* (1976)).

Similar fact evidence for the defence

The vast majority of cases involve the use of similar fact evidence for the prosecution, who is required to show positive probative value. However, there are some cases where the defence may wish to rely on the past misdeeds of a co-accused since this has a relevance to the defendants defence.

In *R v Miller* (1952) the two defendants were accused of customs offences and D1 denied all involvement, stating that it was all the work of D2 who had posed as D1 when he was committing the offences. The offences had stopped for a time whilst D2 was in prison and had restarted on his release. The evidence that D2 had been imprisoned was admissible, notwithstanding that it revealed his bad character. This was relevant to D1's defence and did not just prejudice D2

Where there is no relevance in the previous behaviour to the defendant's defence, but merely an undermining or incriminating of the co-accused by reference to the co-accused's bad character, the evidence is inadmissible, as in *R v Neale* (1977). The defendants were accused of arson, and D1 ran a defence of alibi. D2's previous convictions for arson of a similar kind to that in the offence in question were inadmissible. This was irrelevant to D1's defence of alibi, which did not depend on showing D2 was responsible for the fires.

Use of similar fact evidence

Similar fact evidence can consist of previous convictions, as in *R v Straffen* (1952), or behaviour that is not criminal, as in *R v Butler* (1987) and *R v Barrington* (1981). The defendant does not have to acknowledge that he in fact behaved in that way in the past, as in *R v Rance*

(1975) where the defendant denied the previous corrupt practices that were being used to prove his guilt of the offence charged. The behaviour usually occurs before the offence for which the defendant is charged, but subsequent behaviour can be admitted, as in *R v Geering* (1849) where the defendant accused of murder had deaths subsequent to the murder charged being admitted as evidence.

If the defendant has been convicted of the behaviour, then it may be prejudicial to tell the jury that there has actually been a conviction, and so in *R v Shepherd* (1980) it was suggested that the prosecution should confine themselves to the facts of the behaviour, omitting that it resulted in a conviction. However, the position is not clear and, in s 74(3) PACE 1984, there is provision for admissibility of evidence that the accused has committed an offence if it is relevant to any matter in issue, and he is presumed to have committed the offence on proof of conviction unless the contrary is shown. Whether this impacts on *R v Shepherd* is debatable.

Similar fact evidence in civil cases

Since trial is usually by judge alone there is not the same risk of prejudice through the incorrect assessment of the probative value of the defendant's previous behaviour. There are also not the same dire consequences for the defendant.

In *Mood Music Publishing v De Wolfe* (1976) Lord Denning stated that the test in civil cases was whether the evidence was logically probative, not unduly oppressive to the opponent and proper notice must be given. In this case evidence was admitted that the defendant had been accused of plagiarising songs by other artists in the past to show that his defence of accidental similarity to the plaintiff's work was likely to be a sham.

Sattin v National Union Bank (1978) was a case of negligence where the defendants argued that they had used all due care in their safekeeping of the plaintiff's jewels, and evidence was admitted of other loses from the defendant's bank since this was probative of the sort of care and security arrangements in place.

6 The character of the accused

You should be familiar with the following areas: ✓

- use of character evidence at common law where defendant does not testify
- character evidence where defendant testifies under s 1(f) Criminal Evidence Act 1898
- the shield in s 1(f) and its loss
- the judicial discretion to restrain cross-examination
- the effect of good character

Special rules apply governing the extent to which the prosecution may use the defendant's bad character against him. The rules vary and depend upon whether the defendant testifies or not. As seen in the last chapter, revealing bad character is often prejudicial, and needs to be restricted.

The defendant who does not testify

The common law rules dictate the admissibility of the defendant's character where the defendant does not testify. These rules are more restrictive than the statutory rules applicable when the defendant testifies. At one point defendants would exercise their right to silence precisely because it would ensure that their bad character would not be revealed. Since s 35 Criminal Justice and Public Order Act 1994 this is a less attractive option, as adverse inferences can be drawn from silence. However, the common law rules are still of relevance in the rare case where the defendant does not testify.

The prosecution can accordingly present evidence of the defendant's bad character in the following situations:

- Where the defendant's character is an essential element of the offence

Certain offences are defined in such a way that they of necessity involve the prosecution introducing evidence of the defendant's bad behaviour on other occasions. Such evidence is clearly relevant and admissible. For example, the offence of driving whilst disqualified involves proof of the defendant's prior disqualification, as this is an essential element of the offence and the disqualification is a fact in issue.

- Where the defendant's character is admissible similar fact evidence
  As discussed in the Chapter 5, there are certain cases where the previous behaviour of the defendant has enormous relevance and, because of the positive probative value, the prosecution will be able to use such similar fact evidence against the defendant.
- Where the defendant has raised his good character
  If the defence has involved the calling of witnesses or the asking of questions or making of statements which have been designed to portray the defendant as a person of good character, and as such less likely to have committed the offence, then the prosecution will be allowed to call evidence of bad character in rebuttal. It would obviously be wrong for the jury to have an inaccurate and misleading view of the defendant's character and, since his defence has raised character first, the prosecution will be allowed to present evidence to the contrary.

  Character is indivisible (*R v Winfield* (1939)) so once a defendant puts some aspect of his good character in issue, then the other aspects of his character may be revealed. *R v Butterwasser* (1948) makes it clear that these are the only circumstances in which the character is admissible in common law. The making of imputations about prosecution witnesses was insufficient to make the defendant's character admissible in this case.

Where the defendant testifies

If the defendant testifies, the prosecution not only has the opportunity to reveal his bad character as part of their own case, as detailed above, but they may also question the defendant about his character in cross-examination. The defendant is competent but not compellable in his own defence (s 1 Criminal Evidence Act 1898), but once he enters the witness box he cannot pick and choose which questions to answer. However, testifying would not be an attractive proposition if the defendant could be discredited by reference to his previous character in the same way as ordinary witnesses. Therefore, s 1 contains important provisions that restrict the prosecution in their cross-examination of the defendant.

The s 1(f) shield

Section 1(f) provides that the defendant 'shall not be asked, and if asked, shall not be required to answer, any question tending to show that he has committed, been convicted of or charged with any offences other than that wherewith he is then charged, or is of bad character'. Section 1(f) then goes on to state the circumstances in which this protective shield may be lost.

Thus it can be seen that the prosecution will not be allowed to ask questions which would reveal the defendant's discreditable past behaviour for the first time. In *Jones v DPP* (1962) the House of Lords explained that this shield only existed if the defendant's bad behaviour had not already been revealed to the court. Jones was accused of a murder and he had used an alibi initially that he then admitted was false. He explained that he had initially given the false alibi because he had been 'in trouble' before, and thought he would not be believed. He then changed his story, using another alibi. This second alibi was identical to the one he had used when charged in a rape case some years earlier. The rape had very similar circumstances to the murder, but the prosecution had not explored the similar fact possibility because they did not want the victim to have to relive her ordeal again. The defendant had been convicted of the rape, and the prosecution in the murder trial sought to cross-examine him as to the similarities between his alibi in the murder case and the one he had used in the earlier trial. The House of Lords agreed that the cross-examination should be permitted, although the judgments expressed differing views and reasoning.

From *Jones* it seems to be apparent that if the defendant's bad past has already been revealed whether as part of the prosecution case, or by the defence, then there is no s 1(f) shield. For the shield to exist, the cross-examination must reveal the character *for the first time*. If it has already been revealed, there can be no justification for refusing cross-examination. Such cross-examination would be a relevant exploration of facts already in evidence, and s 1(e) Criminal Evidence Act 1898 provides: 'A person charged and being a witness ... may be asked any question in cross-examination notwithstanding that it may tend to incriminate him.'

Thus in *Jones* the defendant, having already indicated that he had been in trouble before, had no s 1(f) shield, and the similarity between the alibi he was using in the murder trial and the one he had used, falsely, in the rape trial could legitimately be explored by the prosecution. The prosecution did not, however, cross-examine the defendant on the similarities in the details of the two offences.

If the shield exists, it protects the defendant from questions about offences both before and after the offence he is on trial for (*R v Wood* (1920)), and in respect of behaviour that may not be an offence, but may just show bad character, as in *R v Marsh* (1994) concerning a rugby player's bad disciplinary record for violent tackling.

The loss of the shield

If the shield exists it can be lost in one or more of the situations covered by s 1(f)(i)(ii)(iii). There is nothing to restrict cross-examination to one party and not the other in the statute. Therefore, if the shield is lost, it is lost to both the prosecutor and the co-accused, regardless of which subsection applied: *R v Lovett* (1973). However, there is a judicial discretion to restrict prosecution cross-examination, and it will often not be in the co-accused's interests to cross-examine the defendant, even though the shield may have been lost.

Section 1(f)(i): relevance to guilt

Section 1(f)(i) permits cross-examination if 'the proof that he has been committed or been convicted of such other offence is admissible evidence to show that he is guilty of the offence wherewith he is then charged'. Thus it can be seen that the defendant cannot be cross-examined about acquittals or general bad character not amounting to an offence under s 1(f)(i).

Section 1(f)(i) cases are very rare. Usually if the prosecution has evidence that the defendant has been involved in other offences that are relevant to his guilt, they will use such evidence as part of the prosecution case. If it has already been used as part of the prosecution case, there is no s 1(f) shield (*Jones v DPP*), and the cross-examination proceeds under s 1(e) not s 1(f)(i). By not using such evidence, the prosecution runs the risk that the defendant will not testify, thereby ensuring that the bad character does not get revealed. Then if he testifies, the judge may use his discretion under s 78 PACE to prohibit cross-examination that would adversely affect the fairness of proceedings. The prosecution, by taking the defendant by surprise when he is in the witness box, with evidence that if used as part of the prosecution case, he would have had notice of, may be thought to be acting unfairly.

If s 1(f) does apply, it will only apply to the rare kind of cases where the defendant's previous criminality is relevant to his guilt of the offence charged. As seen in the last chapter, similar fact evidence is relevant to the defendant's guilt, and it may also be possible to cross-examine the defendant under s 27(3) Theft Act 1968. In a handling case the accused can be asked about previous convictions for theft or handling within the five years prior to the offence, and possession of stolen goods not beyond the 12 months prior to the offence. This evidence is admissible to tend to show that he knew or believed the goods, that are the subject of the present charge, were stolen. It seems that where a conviction is used the fact of conviction, its date and place and a description of the stolen goods involved may be given in evidence. Cross-examination under s 1(f)(i) is relevant to the defendant's guilt: *R v Hacker* (1995).

Section 1(f)(ii): good character and imputations

The shield may be lost under s 1(f)(ii) by what the defendant says personally or by the way in which the counsel conducts his defence. Section 1(f)(ii) provides for the loss of the shield if 'he has personally or by his advocate asked questions of the witnesses for the prosecution with a view to establishing his own good character, or has given evidence of his own good character, or the nature or conduct of the defence is such as to involve imputations on the character of the prosecutor, or witnesses for the prosecution, or the deceased victim of the offence'.

This last category was inserted by the Criminal Justice and Public Order Act amidst concern that in murder trials defendants were often routinely portraying the deceased in a bad light, as if to excuse the killing, or make it less reprehensible.

Thus it can be seen that s 1(f)(ii) covers what the defendant says, or what his counsel says, and what answers are deliberately elicited from witnesses. However, it seems that where a witness of his own volition, and unsolicited, makes remarks that would seem to fall foul of s 1(f)(ii), the shield will not be lost: *R v Redd* (1923).

Good character
If the defence has involved gratuitous claims of attributes or virtues, designed to show that the defendant is a person of good character and

consequently less likely to commit the offence, then the shield will be lost. Such evidence is not strictly relevant to the facts in issue, and since character is indivisible it would be wrong for the jury to be left with an image of the defendant as a good character if the reality is different. Thus the defence must be careful not to say anything or call witnesses to give evidence of good character unless they are prepared for the shield to be lost.

Claims of religious beliefs (*R v Ferguson* (1909)), family man in honest employment, and not having alcohol for many years (*R v Douglas* (1989)) have been held to be assertions of good character.

However, the shield will not be lost if the defendant gives an explanation of the facts of the case which happen to show the defendant in a good light: *R v Thomson* (1966).

Imputations

The first stage is to check who the remarks in question are referring to. Only remarks derogatory of the prosecutor, prosecution witnesses or deceased victim of the crime will suffice.

If remarks are made about persons who were not called as witnesses by the prosecution, then the shield will not be lost: *R v Lee* (1975). Makers of admissible hearsay statements that are used by the prosecution under ss 23 or 24 Criminal Justice Act count as witnesses for the prosecution, even though they do not give oral evidence.

If this first stage is satisfied, it is then necessary to check if what has been said amounts to an imputation. Distinctions must be drawn between emphatic denials of guilt, which do not cause a loss of shield, however emphatic or rude they may seem to be, and an imputation which is the making of derogatory remarks or allegations of bad behaviour or character. In *R v Rouse* (1994) the witness was called 'a liar' and this was held to be an emphatic denial of guilt. A defendant will frequently need to explain differences between his account of events and that of a prosecution witness. To say that the witness is lying, or mistaken, is not an imputation, even where the defendant goes on to give a reason for the mistake such as the witness being drunk, as in *R v Stanton* (1994), although this may be a question of degree.

However, if the allegation of lying is taken to extremes, as in *R v Rappolt* (1911) (where the witness was accused of being 'such horrible liar, even his own brother won't talk to him') or in *R v Lasseur* (1991) (where the allegation was fabrication to get an accomplice a lighter sentence), the defendant will lose his shield.

It seems that the defendant can deny an element of the offence without this being an imputation, as in *R v Sheean* (1908) where the defendant alleged consent in a rape case without losing his shield.

Most allegations of bad or improper behaviour will usually be imputations, although it is important to remember that each case rests on its facts, and what might once have been an imputation may no longer be regarded as discreditable and no longer an imputation. In *R v Bishop* (1975) the defendant was accused of burglary and explained the presence of his fingerprints in the bedroom of the premises in question by stating that he had been having a homosexual relationship with the occupier. That was held to be an imputation. Allegations that witness have bribed or threatened others (*R v Wright* (1910)) and abuse of prosecution powers to obtain a confession (*R v Jones* (1923)) have been held to be imputations.

The difficult position of the defendant who disputes police versions of events was considered in *R v Britzman* (1983) where it was stated that the shield will be lost if the defence expressly or implicitly make imputations, but that the defence should be able to deny one incident or a short interview without it being an imputation. However, if a number of incidents or interviews, or one lengthy interview, is denied, then this will be an imputation.

If the shield is lost under s 1(f)(ii) then cross-examination is relevant to credit only (*R v Inder* (1977)) and the judge should ensure that the jury is aware that they should not look at the previous offences and infer that the defendant has repeated his earlier criminality.

Section 1(f)(iii): evidence against the co-accused

Section 1(f)(iii) provides that the defendant should lose the protection of s 1(f) shield if 'he has given evidence against any one person charged in the same proceedings'. This sub-section seems to require the defendant to say something in examination in chief or cross-examination that amounts to evidence against the co-accused. Allegations by D's counsel which is not adopted by the defendant should not cause a loss of shield.

In *Murdoch v Taylor* (1965) it was stressed that what counted was the effect of the defendant's evidence, not the intention with which he gave it. Therefore there can be a loss of shield under s 1(f)(iii) though there is no hostility on the part of the defendant towards his co-accused.

It is necessary to see if the defendant has either supported the prosecution case against the co-accused or undermined the co-accused's defence. Supporting the prosecution case normally occurs where the defendant expressly blames or implicates his co-accused. Undermining the co-accused's defence is more subtle, and was considered in *R v Varley* (1982). *Varley* was a robbery case in which the co-accused had admitted participation but ran a defence of duress from the threats of the defendant. The defendant denied any involvement in the robbery. The court said that it was not enough to show that there were inconsistencies between the accounts of the defendant and the co-accused; it was necessary to show that the defendant's denial or inconsistency 'pointed the finger' at the co-accused. In this case, the requirement was satisfied in that the defendant was in essence depriving the co-accused of his defence of duress. Therefore, if the jury were to believe the defendant they would be more likely to convict the co-accused, hence the necessity to permit the cross-examination under s 1(f)(iii), so as to discredit the defendant.

In *R v Bruce* (1975) the defendant and co-accused were on trial for conspiracy to rob. The co-accused had admitted that there was a conspiracy, but denied being a party; the defendant denied that there was a conspiracy at all. This denial by the defendant was inconsistent with the co-accused's defence, but it did not amount to evidence against the co-accused. If the jury were to believe the defendant they would be more likely to acquit the co-accused than convict, as they would conclude that there was no conspiracy. Therefore, the defendant had not given evidence against a co-accused and the co-accused conviction was not more likely.

If the shield is lost to the co-accused there is no judicial discretion to prevent cross-examination (*R v Varley; Murdoch v Taylor*); the only limit will be relevance.

Cross-examination under s 1(f)(iii) is relevant to credibility, ie to show that the defendant is not to be believed on his oath.

The judicial discretion

The shield may be lost both to the prosecution and co-accused under s 1(f)(i)(ii) and s 1(f)(iii). It has already been noted that there is no judicial discretion to prevent the co-accused from cross-examining the defendant; it is important that an accused is free to present his defence in the best way possible, even though that may harm someone with whom he is on trial.

The same reasoning does not apply to the prosecution and in *Selvey v DPP* (1970) the court emphasised that the judge should consider whether or not to exercise his discretion in favour of 'fairness to the accused'. *Selvey* was a case where the defendant lost the shield through the making of imputations on a prosecution witness (s 1(f)(ii)). The defendant was accused of assault and argued that the allegation had been falsely made by the witness whose homosexual advances the defendant had rebuffed.

Section 78 PACE provides that evidence tendered by the prosecution may be excluded if to admit it in all the circumstances would 'adversely affect the fairness of proceedings'. The following guidelines may be drawn from the cases but, remember, ultimately each case depends upon its own facts, and it is important to take into account how strong the prosecution case is, as well as the prejudicial effect of admitting the evidence.

Guidelines

The shield is more likely to be lost if the situation arises from deliberate defence tactics, than if it arises as a result of the defendant making remarks in cross-examination. Allowances will be made for the strain of cross-examination: *R v Britzman* (1983). Greater leniency is also shown where the defence were forced into making the imputation, as it is a necessary part of their defence: *R v Bishop* (1975); *Selvey v DPP* (1970).

Where the shield is lost through the making of imputations, the prosecution's strongest argument is the 'tit for tat' argument in *Selvey* that, if the defendant has made imputations, it is only right that the court should know what kind of man the defendant is. It would be wrong for the court to be under the impression that the defendant is a man of good character, if in reality he is not.

An important consideration is perhaps to look at the kind of offences the defendant has committed in the past. If they are very old offences, there may be an argument for saying that they should not be used to discredit the defendant many years later. Spent offences under the Rehabilitation of Offenders Act 1974 should not be referred to without leave from the trial judge, and such leave should only be given if it is in the interest of justice. Old offences that were committed when the defendant was under 14 cannot be referred to once the defendant reaches 21: s 16 Children and Young Persons Act 1963.

If the person's convictions are for offences that bear a close similarity to the present offence, there is a risk that, if cross-examination is allowed, the jury will get the impression that the defendant has a propensity to behave in the way alleged, and is repeating his previous criminal behaviour. This may be an argument in favour of denying the cross-examination (*Maxwell v DPP* (1935)) or, in the very least, requiring a strong judicial warning to the jury that the cross-examination affects credibility and does not to go the defendant's guilt (*R v McLeod* (1994)).

The traditional view is that a previous offence of dishonesty impacts on the defendant's credibility and makes him less believable as a witness. Consequently, it is common for offences of dishonesty to be the subject of cross-examination. On occasions the defendant's record contains details of offences that may shock and prejudice the jury against him. This is a particular concern where the offences are sexual or involve child victims, and may be the basis of preventing cross-examination: *R v Watts* (1983). However, there is no absolute rule that cross-examination on prejudicial offences will be prevented, nor on an offence that bears a similarity to the offence charged (*R v Powell* (1985)); it all depends on the circumstances of the case. Cross-examination may be allowed or prevented absolutely, or there is the possibility that the judge will allow cross-examination in relation to some offences, but not others.

Nature of cross-examination

Cross-examination under s 1(f)(ii) and s 1(f)(iii) is relevant to credibility only, and therefore it is important to avoid cross-examination that might suggest propensity to behaviour in a particular way thus pointing to guilt: *R v France* (1979). This does not mean that the prosecution is limited to cross-examination on the mere fact of the conviction but they should avoid unnecessary and distracting cross-examination on factual similarities between the past offences and the present offence. It is wrong to explore similarities with a view to encouraging the jury to infer repetition of facts pointing to guilt, but it is acceptable to explore factual similarities that relate to credibility. For example, whether the accused pleaded not guilty and was disbelieved on his oath or whether he had run the same false defence or alibi in the past would be correctly explored: *R v McLeod* (1994).

Cross-examination about acquittals

Whilst it is relatively easy to see how convictions for previous offences may be relevant to a defendant's credibility, this is not so easily illustrated where the cross-examination is proposed in relation to acquittals. The s 1(f) shield prohibits cross-examination about acquittals, since these are offences the defendant was charged with. However, if the shield is lost, then technically cross-examination may sometimes be permitted.

Section 1(f)(i) does not allow cross-examination about acquittals; as acquittals should not be relevant to a defendant's guilt.

If the shield is lost under s 1(f)(ii) and s 1(f)(iii) it will be necessary for the cross-examining party to demonstrate that the acquittal has a relevance to the defendant's credibility.

In *Maxwell v DPP* (1935) the defendant, who was accused of illegal abortion, lost his shield by asserting that he was of a good, moral character who would not perform such illegal abortions. The prosecution wished to ask him about previous acquittals for illegal abortions. Such cross-examination should not be allowed. The acquittals did not show he performed illegal abortions, nor did they affect his good character. It would be highly prejudicial to allow cross-examination, as it might suggest that to the jury that the defendant had 'got away with it before', and should not do so again.

However, if a defendant loses the shield by claiming to have a good reputation, this may allow cross-examination on acquittals. The defendant's reputation is his standing in the eyes of others, and this can be affected by charges being brought, even though they may result in an acquittal. Thus the defendant is painting an inaccurate picture of his reputation, which can be corrected by cross-examination. In *R v Wildman* (1934) the defendant argued that he had a good reputation for honesty, opening the way for cross-examination about two previous convictions and acquittals for dishonesty offences.

Good character

A defendant in a criminal case is permitted to call witnesses to give evidence of the defendant's general reputation amongst those who know him. However, to avoid wasting time and distracting the jury, *R v Rowton* (1865) laid down the rule that the witness could not give evidence of specific credible acts by the defendant. In *Rowton* evidence of a schoolmaster's general reputation was admissible at his trial for offences of indecency, but the witness was prevented from giving his own opinion of the defendant and details of the defendant's past good deeds.

Modern practice is to allow a little more flexibility than suggested in *R v Rowton*, and defendants are allowed to state that they have no convictions, and witnesses are frequently permitted to state their own opinion of the defendant, although this is not an entitlement, but rather depends on judicial practice.

R v Rowton was used in *R v Redgrave* (1981) to prevent a witness giving evidence of the defendant's heterosexual relationships where the defendant was accused of a homosexual offence. Such tendencies are not relevant to whether the defendant committed the crime and could only be examples of so called 'creditable' behaviour prohibited by *R v Rowton*.

The evidential value of good character

A defendant of good character is considered to be more credible than a defendant of bad character (*R v Falconer Atlee* (1973)), and consequently his good character may make his testimony more believable. However, possession of good character goes beyond credibility, and may mean that the defendant is less likely to commit the offence in question: *R v Bryant* (1979); *R v Berrada* (1990). Of course, this is not an absolute defence – every criminal started off at one time as a person of good character!

The good character direction

In *R v Vye, Wise and Stephenson* (1993) the Court of Appeal gave guidance as to the type of direction a trial judge should give when the defendant's good character needs to be explained to the jury.

The first limb direction, that the defendant's good character makes him more credible, must be given where the defendant testifies at trial and has made admissible out of court statements to the police or others. In such cases the jury need to know whether the defendant's word can be relied on. A first limb direction is not needed in respect of out of court statements that are totally exculpatory (*R v Aziz* (1995)) as such statements are not admissible to prove the truth of their contents. No first limb direction is given therefore where the defendant remains silent throughout.

A second limb direction is given in all cases of good character, regardless of whether the defendant testifies.

The *R v Vye* direction can be tailored to meet the needs of the particular case, and common sense will often dictate exactly what form the direction should take. For example, if no reference has been made to old spent offences then the judge should not say that the defendant has no convictions, since that is misleading, but it would be right to say that the defendant is of good character.

If the defendant has no convictions, but there is a question mark over his character because of allegations of dishonesty or bad behaviour, the judge will need to consider carefully how to direct the jury. It will be rare that no *Vye* direction will be given; however, it will need to be modified to take into account the alleged misconduct: *R v Aziz, R v Zoppola-Barraza* (1994).

If the defendant pleads guilty to some counts on the indictment, but not on others, it will usually not be possible to treat him as a person of good character: *R v Challenger* (1994). However, he may be given credit for having pleaded guilty, with a possible inference that this makes his not guilty plea on the other counts more credible. However, if the indictment contains counts in the alternative, then a plea of guilty to the lesser offence may not necessarily prevent a *Vye* good character direction: *R v Teasdale* (1993). For example, a defendant accused of murder and manslaughter in alternative courts may plead not guilty to murder but guilty to manslaughter because of provocation. If he has no other convictions, he may be treated as being less likely to commit murder, notwithstanding his plea of guilty to manslaughter.

The defendant of good character on trial with others of bad character

In *R v Vye* the Court of Appeal made it clear that a defendant of good character is entitled to a direction on that in his favour, even if he is on trial with others of bad character, who may be damaged by implication by the good character direction. This is a further example of the principle that an accused should be free to present his defence in as effective a way as possible, even though this may damage a fellow co-accused.

The Law Commission Consultation Paper No 141

The Law Commission issued a consultation paper entitled 'Evidence in Criminal Proceedings: Previous Misconduct of a Defendant' in 1996, inviting comments on possible changes to the rules on admissibility of character evidence in criminal trials. The Law Commission thought that the defendant ought to be able to adduce evidence of his good character and receive a measure of protection from his bad character being revealed. The prosecution should be able to use bad character as part of its case if such evidence is relevant to a specific issue and any prejudicial effect is outweighed by its probative value. This would equate with what is now termed similar fact evidence, although it was proposed that guidelines should be given to assist the court. The loss of the s 1(f) shield in respect of the defendant who testifies was the subject of recommended changes. First, the shield should be lost not only where there is an express claim of good character, but also an implied one, such as the wearing of a dog collar, or possibly a regimental tie? The shield should also be lost where the defendant calls a witness to testify inaccurately about the defendant's good character. In relation to the making of imputations the recommended changes would work in the defendant's favour, as he would only lose his shield if what he said about the witness did not relate to the way the witness had behaved in relation to the offence or investigation in question. Thus allegations of police impropriety in the conduct of the investigation would not involve a loss of shield. The loss of shield under s 1(f)(iii) should only arise if what was said did not relate to the co-accused's conduct in relation to the offence or the investigation of the offence. Thus the effect of these proposals would be to give a greater degree of protection to defendants than they presently enjoy. It remains to be seen whether any changes are forthcoming.

7 Corroboration and care warnings

What is corroboration?

Corroboration has a technical meaning, and has been the subject of a great deal of academic criticism. In *R v Baskerville* (1916) corroboration was defined as 'independent testimony which affects the accused by connecting or tending to connect him with the crime'. Thus corroborative evidence must satisfy the following requirements:

- Admissible evidence in its own right
  Evidence must be admissible in its own right before it can be considered to corroborate other evidence.
- Independent evidence
  The evidence must come from a source that is independent or different from the evidence requiring corroboration. Thus previous consistent statements by the witness cannot amount to corroboration, since they derive from the same, not an independent, source: *R v Whitehead* (1929). This was a case where a recent complaint, admissible as a previous consistent statement was not corroborative of the complainant's testimony since 'it proceeded from the girl herself, it was merely the girl's story at secondhand. In order that evidence may amount to corroboration it must be extraneous to the witness who is to be corroborated'.

Although the complaint will not qualify as corroboration, the independent observation of the victim's distress by the witness can amount to corroboration (*R v Chauhan* (1981)) although the weight to be given to it will vary with the circumstances of the case (*R v Redpath* (1962)) and whether the victim has had the opportunity to simulate a fake distress.

* Connect the defendant with the crime

For the evidence to be corroborative it must incriminate the defendant in the commission of the offence; ie support the prosecution case on all the live issues: *James v R* (1970). Thus medical evidence indicating rape cannot be corroboration if the defendant's identity is in issue, unless the forensic evidence can point to the defendant being the attacker.

It would seem that pieces of evidence that do not individually amount to corroboration can be added together, and if the effect is then to incriminate the defendant on all the live issues, then there is cumulative corroboration: *R v Hills* (1987). Corroboration was said to come from 'a combination of pieces of circumstantial evidence, each innocuous on its own, which together tend to show that the defendant committed the crime'.

Two witnesses who require corroboration can corroborate each other's testimony (*DPP v Kilbourne* (1973)) provided there is no collusion. Such mutual corroboration is often a feature in many of the similar fact cases, although following the Criminal Justice and Public Order Act 1994 abolition of the need for a corroboration warning, corroboration is unlikely to be a major feature of the law of evidence.

Corroboration required by law

The vast majority of offences do not require corroboration, and a conviction is in theory possible on one piece of uncorroborated evidence. However, the following offences require corroboration before a conviction can be obtained:

* treason;
* perjury;
* speeding.

For all other offences there is no legal requirement for corroboration.

Corroboration warnings

Under the old law, there were certain categories of witness in respect of whom judges were required to give the jury a corroboration warning. This warning told the jury of the dangers of convicting on that witness's evidence alone and of the desirability of looking for corroboration. Corroboration was then explained to the jury and they were told what evidence in the case was capable of being corroborative. It was still open to the jury to convict without corroboration.

This had the effect of possibly undermining the evidence of witnesses falling into those categories, even though there was no cause for concern on the facts of the case.

The categories of witness requiring corroboration warnings under the old law were:

* Children

  Now s 34 Criminal Justice Act 1988 as amended provides that the judge no longer needs to warn the jury about the dangers of convicting on the uncorroborated evidence of the child.

* Accomplices

  An accomplice is someone who testifies for the prosecution and who was a participant in the offence for which the defendant is charged, or a participant in a similar fact offence, or a receiver in the case of a thief: *Davies v DPP* (1954). A defendant who gives evidence in his own defence is not an accomplice: *R v Barnes* (1940). It used to be thought that an accomplice may testify for a variety of motives, not all of them consistent with telling the truth. Consequently, the jury were warned about the dangers of his evidence. The accomplice corroboration warning requirement was abolished by s 32 Criminal Justice and Public Order Act 1994.

* Complainants in sexual offences

  A warning also used to be given about the dangers of relying on the uncorroborated evidence of a complainant. This routinely undermined the evidence of a victim of sexual offences by suggesting that such complaints are easily made, difficult to rebut and that there is a risk complainants may be acting out of a desire for revenge, hysteria or shame.

  The requirement for such a warning was abolished by s 32(1) Criminal Justice and Public Order Act 1994. In *R v Makanjuola* (1995) the Court of Appeal considered the effect of s 32(1) CJPOA and concluded that it had abolished the requirement for a routine corroboration warning just because the witness fell into the category of accomplice or complainant in sexual cases. This is now replaced by a judicial discretion to warn if on the facts of the particular case the judge feels that that is evidence showing cause for concern about the evidence of a particular witness. This discretion will not be lightly interfered with by the Court of Appeal and will only give a successful ground of appeal if no reasonable judge would have failed to warn the jury.

If a warning is given its nature and content will vary from case to case. A technical corroboration warning is unnecessary, most cases will just involve a warning to be careful, with the possibility of looking for supporting evidence.

Care warnings

Although it is no longer likely that corroboration warnings will be encountered very frequently, there are cases where the judge is required by law, or has a discretion, to warn the jury to be careful about the evidence of a witness. The following are examples of such cases:

- Children
  Although there is no longer a need to look for corroboration, and although the law has gone a great way to facilitate the giving of evidence by children, there can still be dangers in relying on a child's evidence in some cases. Some children do have difficulty in distinguishing between fact and fiction, and can be confused or misinterpret what they have seen. In such cases it might be appropriate for the judge to warn the jury about the possible problems: *DPP v Hester* (1973).
- Accomplices
  See s 32(1) CJPOA 1994 and *R v Makanjuola* (1995).
- Complainants in sexual cases
  See s 32(1) CJPOA and *R v Makanjuola*.
- Witnesses with an 'axe to grind'
  In *R v Beck* (1982) it was suggested that where a witness may have reasons of his own for testifying, such as a grudge, or to excuse his own behaviour, the judge could exercise discretion and warn the jury to 'proceed with caution'.
- Evidence from mentally ill offenders and persons in secure mental institutions
  In *R v Spencer* (1987) the House of Lords thought that the judge could give a care warning in relation to the dangers of relying on the

evidence of a witness who was a patient or offender at a secure mental institution.

- Confessions by the mentally handicapped
  Section 77 PACE 1984 requires the trial judge to warn the jury about the need for caution in convicting a mentally handicapped defendant on the basis of confession made in the absence of an independent adult. Mental handicap is defined in the section to mean arrested or incomplete development of mind, and that includes significant impairment of intelligence and social functioning. This is an absolute requirement where the prosecution case depends wholly or substantially on such a confession.

- Identification evidence
  Once the prosecution case against the accused depends wholly or substantially on disputed identification evidence from one or more witnesses, the judge is required to apply the *R v Turnbull* (1977) guidelines. These guidelines require the judge to warn the jury about the dangers of identification evidence, and in some cases to direct the jury on the desirability of looking for supporting evidence. This is considered in detail in the next chapter.

8 Identification evidence

General descriptions

Wherever a witness observes the commission of a crime, they will be asked by the police to give a general description of the offender. This general description may be circumstantial evidence against the accused if he fits the description given. The more closely he fits the description and the more unusual the features, the greater the weight of the circumstantial evidence against him. Such evidence does not usually give cause for concern; it is as reliable or unreliable as any other eye witness evidence.

Identification of the accused

However, if a witness goes beyond giving a general description of the offender and goes on to identify the defendant as the actual person the witness saw commit the offence, then there is a need for caution. Mistaken identification is common and, as the Court of Appeal observed in *R v Turnbull* (1977), honest witnesses are easily mistaken, yet none the less appear to be convincing witnesses to the jury. Since there is an enormous risk of miscarriage of justice through wrongful identification judges are obliged to follow the guidelines in *R v Turnbull* and give the jury a special warning wherever the prosecution case against the accused consists wholly or substantially of disputed identification evidence.

The application of the *R v Turnbull* guidelines

R v Turnbull (1977) applies where there is the possibility of mistakenly identifying the accused; it is of no application where the defence contends that the identification is maliciously wrong: *R v Cape* (1996). If the defendant admits being at the scene and merely disputes the nature of what he was observed doing then there is no need for a *Turnbull* direction (*R v Oakwell* (1978)), as for example, where the defendant argues the witness mistook his giving the victim something for the defendant striking the victim. However, if the scene is very crowded and in the commotion there is a risk that the eye witness may be mistaken in thinking that the defendant is the member of the crowd responsible for the offence, *R v Slater* (1995) says a *R v Turnbull* warning will be called for.

   R v Turnbull only applies where the prosecution case depends wholly or substantially on mistaken identification evidence. If the prosecution case against the defendant is exceptionally strong, and the identification evidence is merely a small, almost insignificant, part then there may be no need for a warning.

Failure to follow

If the case is one where the judge should have given a *Turnbull* warning, then his failure to do so will be a good ground of appeal: *R v Breslin* (1984).

Assessing the quality of the evidence

In order for the judge to determine exactly what approach he should adopt in directing the jury on the identification evidence, the judge must form a view as to the strengths of the evidence. In *R v Turnbull* the Court of Appeal gave an indication of the kind of factors that affect the quality of the evidence:

- length of observation: great concern exists where the identification is made after a fleeting glimpse of the offender. Usually, the longer the period of observation, the stronger the evidence;
- distance: the closer the witness was to the offender, the better; the further away, the greater the possibility of mistake;
- lighting: consider the time of day or night and the quality of light. Sunlight/moonlight/shadows/artificial light all affect the quality of the evidence;
- obstructions: was the witness' view impeded in anyway, by passing traffic, trees blocking the view, by the defendant covering his face or blindfolding the witness;
- state of victim: greater weight will be given to identification evidence from reliable witnesses. Bad eyesight, drunkenness, drug addiction or concussion could all adversely affect the quality of the evidence;
- does the witness know the offender: most concern exists where the eye witness identifies a stranger, someone he has never seen before the offence. Generally, recognition of a person known to the witness is stronger, although mistakes are possible and it is necessary to consider how well the two are known to one another, and whether there was any special reason for the witness to remember the person;
- when was the description given: the shorter the interval of time between witnessing the incident and going on to identify the defendant, the better;
- conformity to description: it is necessary to look at the description given and see how far the defendant conforms to the description and whether he differs from it in any material respect.

Directing the jury

Once the judge has considered the quality of the identification evidence he must then decide how to direct the jury in relation to it. If the quality of the evidence is very good then it can be safely left to the jury with just a warning to them on the inherent dangers of identification evidence. If the quality of the identification evidence is very poor then it should be withdrawn from the jury if there is no supporting evidence. In *R v Daley* (1993) the defendant was purportedly identified by a witness who had remained hidden throughout the robbery and who had only caught a fleeting glimpse of the attacker from a distance. There was no support, and so this could not be safely left to the jury.

If there are some strengths to the evidence, but it is not exceptionally strong then it can be left to the jury but with a full *Turnbull* warning. This involves telling the jury of the inherent dangers of identification evidence, including the fact that mistakes are common, and that honest witnesses may be mistaken but nevertheless convincing. The judge will bring to the jury's attention the strengths and weaknesses of the identification evidence in the case. The desirability of looking for support for the identification evidence is explained, together with an explanation of what evidence exists, that could be regarded as supporting evidence.

Supporting evidence

Evidence supports identification if it tends to suggest that the identification may be correct and reduces the possibility of mistaken identification. The evidence does not have to meet the technical requirement of corroboration, but any evidence that is corroborative will certainly amount to support.

Support may be derived from one or more of the following sources:
- Other witnesses
  Support from witness A's identification of the defendant can come from the identification of the defendant by witness B (*R v Weeder* (1980)) provided that the judge points out to the jury that a number of witnesses may make the same mistake.
- Defendant's lies
  If the defendant has given an alibi that can be shown to be false, or lied on some other matter this may support identification. However, it is important to remember that there are lots of reasons why defendants may lie, and only lies that meet the *R v Lucas* (1981) criteria of being deliberate lies on material matters made to avoid detection of guilt and no other reason will support identification evidence.
- The defendant's incriminatory behaviour under the Criminal Justice and Public Order Act 1994
  The CJPOA provides that in certain circumstances adverse inferences can be drawn from certain aspects of the defendant's behaviour. It may be that in appropriate cases the inference can be drawn that the defendant's behaviour supports the witness' identification of him. Section 34 deals with a failure to mention facts that are relied on in the defendant's defence; s 35 deals with a failure to testify at trial; and ss 36 and 37 deal with a failure to account for possession of incriminatory items and presence in incriminatory places. These sections are dealt with in more detail in Chapter 14.

The defendant's failure to provide samples

Section 62 PACE governs the police power in relation to intimate samples. Intimate samples include blood, semen, and other body fluids, dental impressions, pubic hair, and swabs of body orifices other than the mouth. The taking of such samples require a superintendent's supervision and can only be requested if there are reasonable grounds for believing that the suspect is involved in a recordable offence, ie one punishable by imprisonment, and that the sample would tend to confirm or deny his involvement. The suspect must be asked for his consent, and no sample is possible if he refuses. However, s 62 provides that he should be warned that his failure to consent may lead to adverse inferences being drawn. This would include the inference that the identification was correct. Section 61 governs fingerprinting and s 63 governs non-intimate samples which include saliva, mouth swabs, hair, footprints or other impressions of parts of the body other than the hand. Such samples can be taken without the suspect's consent using reasonable force, and there is no provision in the statute for the drawing of adverse inferences from a refusal.

Forensic evidence

There may be ways in which modern forensic science can link a defendant to a crime. DNA testing enables a good genetic profile to be drawn up of the offender, and there may be links through the presence of blood stains, hair, particles of clothing, etc, or by checking the new national register.

Similar fact convictions

If, when the witness identifies the accused it is discovered that he has previous similar fact convictions, this will tend to suggest that the identification is correct: *DPP v Kilbourne* (1973). Remember, it is not enough that the defendant has convictions for similar offences, they must be similar fact evidence, ie have positive probative value in the form of striking similarity.

Esoteric circumstantial evidence

On occasions a witness describes some feature about the defendant or his possessions and the witness could only really know this if their story was true and they were correct in their identification of the defendant. Such evidence will qualify as support. In *R v McInnes* (1960) a child complained she had been indecently assaulted by the defendant. She described the defendant and went on to identify him, but she also described in detail the type of car her attacker used, including details about discarded sweet wrappers inside the car. The car matched the description exactly, and this was esoteric circumstantial evidence supporting her identification of the defendant. The chance of identifying the defendant and him having the same unusual type of car was inexplicable on the basis of coincidence.

Identification procedures and Code D of PACE 1984

Identification evidence has inherent risks, and is very easily contaminated and rendered unreliable. To ensure that the quality of identification evidence is preserved, and to ensure fairness to the defendant, Code D of the PACE codes of the practice lays down detailed rules resulting in the procedures by which identification evidence should be obtained. A breach of the codes may result in exclusion of the evidence under s 78 PACE if to admit the evidence would adversely affect the fairness of proceedings. The more serious the breach, the more likely the evidence will be excluded, but there is no guarantee that minor breaches will lead to exclusion.

The initial description

Before the eye witness can take part in any identification procedures a written record must be made of their original description of the offender: para 2 Code D.

Procedures where the identify of the suspect is known to the police

The conduct of identifying procedures is the responsibility of the identifying officer, who must be a uniformed officer of at least the rank of inspector who is not involved in the investigation (para 2.2).
The methods of identification available are:
- the identification parade;
- group identification;

- video film;
- confrontation.

1 The identification parade

An identity parade should be held where there is disputed identification by the suspect, or if the investigating officer considers it would be helpful. The suspect must consent to the holding of the parade (para 2:3). There is no need to hold a parade if this would not be practicable to get enough other people who resemble the suspect to take part because of the suspect's unusual appearance or for some other reason (para 2:4). There is also no need to hold a parade if, through fear of the witness or some other reason, a group identification is more satisfactory (para 2:7) or if a video film identification would be more satisfactory (para 2:10). The burden of proving that the parade was not practicable will be on the prosecution, and mere inconvenience does not suffice.

Notice must be given to the suspect both orally and in writing of his rights regarding the parade (para 2:15 and 2:16) and the suspect must sign to indicate whether he is willing to participate or not. The notice will inform the suspect that the parade is being held, the procedures to be employed, his entitlement to free legal advice and to have a solicitor or friend present, any special arrangements that may be appropriate for juveniles and the mentally handicapped, that he can refuse his consent, but that if he does so this can be used in evidence against him and that the police may organise another, possibly covert, identification procedure. He is also informed that if he changes his appearance this may be given in evidence and can lead to other forms of identification being used (para 2:15).

The procedures for the conduct of the parade are contained in Annex A. Before the parade takes place the suspect must be given the opportunity to have a solicitor or friend present and the conduct of the parade should be in their presence, sight and hearing. The original description given by the witness should be given to the suspect together with details of any other material released to the media to trace the suspect.

The suspect must be reminded of the procedures and cautioned and asked if he has any objection. He can select his own position in the line up, which should consist of at least eight other persons of similar description. Two suspects of similar appearance can stand in the same line up provided there are at least 12 others present. No more than two suspects should be in any line up. If there is more than one suspect then different members of the public should be used if there are different line ups. Positions in the line up should be clearly numbered. The parade can take place in a normal room or one with a screen, but all unauthorised persons should be excluded.

Each witness should be brought in one at a time and be told that the person he saw may or may not be on the parade. No attempt should be made to prompt the witness, nor should he be told if anyone else has made a positive identification. Witnesses should not be allowed to communicate with one another, nor be reminded of any photograph or description of the suspect, nor see members of the parade or the suspect before or after the parade. The witness should be asked to carefully look at the line up and identify the suspect by number. If the witness can not identify by appearance alone, he can ask for the members of the parade to adopt a particular pose or to speak, although he needs to be reminded that they have similar physical, not other, attributes.

The suspect must be informed of the witness' identification and the witness should be asked if he has seen any media material on the case. His answer should be recorded, and once the last witness has left the suspect can be asked for his comments. Full records must be kept, and a photograph or video of the parade should be taken. Copies will be provided to the suspect or his solicitor.

2 Group identification

A group identification is where the suspect is identified from amongst an informal group of people, whether in a building or public place. This can be with the suspect's consent, or covertly if he has refused to comply with an identification parade or group identification. The safeguards for an identification parade should be complied with in so far as they are practicable (Annex E), in order to ensure fairness to the suspect. Again, a photograph or video of the group identification should be made if practicable, proper records maintained and the suspect given the opportunity to have a solicitor or friend present if he has agreed to take part. Exceptionally group identifications can take place at a police station if for reasons of safety, security or practicality it is not reasonable to hold them elsewhere.

3 Video film identification

A video film of the suspect may be used if the investigating officer considers it the most satisfactory course of action because the suspect does not consent to an identification parade or group identification or for some other reason. The suspect should be asked for his consent, but the officer has a discretion to use video films if the suspect refuses consent. The procedures are in Annex B. The film must contain scenes of the suspect and at least eight others of similar appearance doing similar things or in similar poses. The film must be made in such a way that each person is identifiable by number, and if practicable the film should be shown to the suspect and his solicitor before it is shown to witnesses. A representative of the suspect should be allowed to be present when the video is shown to the witness and such protective rules as apply to identification parades also apply to video film identifications. There should be no prompting or suggestions made to the witness and proper records must be kept.

4 Confrontation

If there is no parade, group identification or video identification then the suspect can be confronted by the witness. This procedure does not require the suspect's consent and is governed by Annex C. The witness is told that the person may or may not be the person he saw, and is asked 'is this the person' when confronting the suspect. Normally, confrontation takes place at the police station, and a solicitor or friend should be present unless this would cause unreasonable delay. Safeguards mentioned in relation to identification parades apply in so far as practicable.

Where the identify of the suspect is not known

The methods of identification available are:
- street identification;
- photographs, photofits, etc;
- media coverage;

1 Street identification (para 2:17)

If the suspect's identity is unknown then the witness can be taken to a neighbourhood or place to see if he can see the person he saw. The witness should not be prompted and a record should be made of the witness' original description if practicable before any street identification, and a record should be made of any street identification.

2 Photographs, photofits, etc

A witness should not be shown photographs etc if the identity of the suspect is known to the police and he is available to take part on a parade (Para 2:18). If the suspect's identity is not known then the photos etc may be shown in accordance with Annex D. The showing of photographs should be supervised by a sergeant or higher ranking officer, although the actual showing can be done by a police officer or employee of the police. The original description must be recorded before photos are shown and only one witness at a time should be shown the photographs. There should be at least 12 photographs and the witness should be told that the person may or may not be in the photos. There should be no prompting, records should be kept of any identification and the photos should not be shown to other witnesses and an identification parade should be held later.

3 Media coverage

Nothing in Code D prevents the police from releasing material to the media in the form of photos, films, photofits and the like to try to ensure the public recognise the suspect and that he can be traced. If such material is later shown to particular witnesses, this should be done as far as possible on an individual basis.

Other identification methods at trial

1 Voice recognition

It is possible to play a tape to the jury to see if they can recognise the defendant's voice (*R v Bentum* (1989)), although it is advisable to call an expert in voice recognition to confirm the voice as that of the defendant. If a witness gives evidence that he overheard remarks that he believes were made by the accused, then the judge may warn the jury of the possibility of mistaking the accused's voice: *R v Deenick* (1992).

2 Video/security films of incidents

In many cases the likeness of the offender has been captured on a security film. Provided the quality is not too poor, the jury can be shown the film and asked to consider whether the person in the film is the defendant: *Kajala v Noble* (1982). It is also possible to call someone who knew the defendant to state that they recognised him on the film, even if that person is a police officer: *R v Caldwell* (1994).

3 Facial mapping

If the offender's appearance has changed through ageing, or growing a beard, change in hairstyle etc, then it may be possible to call an expert in facial mapping: *R v Stockwell* (1993).

9 The rule against hearsay

You should be familiar with the following areas:

- definition of hearsay
- kinds of statements covered by rule
- statements tendered for truth of contents
- statements tendered for other relevant purpose

Introduction

A great deal of the English law of evidence appears to be pre-occupied with the rule against hearsay and the exceptions to such a rule. Hearsay evidence is when a prior statement, made before the present court proceedings, is tendered as evidence to prove the truth of its contents. The rule extends to statements made previously by the witness himself, or by others.

In the case of prior statements by the witness himself, they are no more likely to be true than prior statements made by others. Repetition is as consistent with lying as with telling the truth.

Prior statements made by others are excluded because the witness has no personal knowledge of the matters he is recounting. Even if the witness is truthful and reliable, his evidence is tainted by the possible unreliability of the person or document relating the events to him. It is also difficult for an opponent to properly test hearsay evidence by cross-examination, with the risk that it will be accorded weight that is disproportionate to its probative value.

However, reference can be made to prior statements for any relevant purpose other than the truth of its contents. Such evidence is termed non-hearsay, original or circumstantial evidence.

The rule is of wide application and it is important to look carefully at the real nature of evidence being tendered to see if it consists of the tendering of a prior statement. If the only purpose of the evidence is to establish the truth of the contents, then the evidence will be hearsay and inadmissible, unless it falls within an exception to the rule against hearsay.

Over the years, exceptions to the rule against hearsay have developed, initially at common law and more recently by way of statute. The greatest relaxation has occurred in civil cases, where the fact that trial is usually by judge alone has justified the admission of hearsay, subject to notice requirements: Civil Evidence Act 1995. The Law Commission has been active in suggesting the reforms that led to this recent Act, and, in their Consultation Paper No 138, they make recommendations in relation to reform of the rule against hearsay in criminal cases.

Testing whether the evidence is hearsay

Evidence is hearsay if the following two questions are answered in the affirmative:
• Is there a prior statement?
• Is the statement tendered to prove the truth of its contents?

1 Is there a prior statement?
The rule against hearsay covers prior statements or assertions by anyone, including the witness themselves. The rule extends to any method of communicating information, whether orally, visually, by words, gestures or documents.

In *R v Gibson* (1887) the witness gave evidence that they had been told by a woman that a person who threw a stone had entered a particular house, and that the woman had then pointed to the house. Both the oral remark by the woman and her gesture of pointing were prior statements, which were being tendered for their truth, and were consequently hearsay.

In *Myers v DPP* (1965) the House of Lords held that documentary records of car parts and their serial numbers was hearsay evidence. The documents were prior statements and since they were being tendered for the truth of their contents, they were hearsay. The House of Lords cautioned against the temptation to categorise evidence as not being hearsay in order to avoid the strictness of the rule, but this is not an approach that courts have always followed!

A controversial decision in *R v Cook* (1987) was followed in *R v Constantinou* (1990). These cases concerned the admissibility of photofit evidence, which consists of a visual impression of a criminal's appearance drawn up by a photofit artist, or now by use of computerised videofit programs, at the direction of an identifying witness. The court held that photofits were a form of evidence *sui generis*, ie of a special nature akin to a photograph, albeit imperfect. As such the photofits were admissible, and were not caught by the rule against hearsay.

This decision may be justifiable where the witness who helped produce the photofit testifies. The photofit will then be judged in terms of its quality against the witness and how well they testify. Since it relates to identification it would be a form of previous consistent statement that would be admissible, although the court rejected the need for this argument in *R v Cook*.

However, it is difficult to see how a photofit can be admissible if the person who helped draw it up is not testifying. In *Sparks v R* (1964) a child's description of her attacker to her mother was inadmissible as hearsay evidence when recounted by the mother. The mother's evidence consists of her relating a prior statement by the child for the purpose of showing that the contents of the child's statement was true. This was hearsay, even though it would have assisted the defence, and was inadmissible. It could not be admitted as a previous consistent statement relating to identification either, as the child was too young to give evidence.

If the child's oral description to her mother was inadmissible hearsay, it is difficult to see how admissibility of a photofit drawn by the same child could be justified. The photofit is subject to the same concerns of unreliability as the oral description, and cannot be properly tested by cross-examination. In addition, whilst a photograph depends upon the mechanical operation of a camera, with no human input, the photofit depends entirely upon human input and recollection.

This line of argument could also prove dangerous, since if a photofit is admissible to prove the likeness of the criminal for the prosecution, then a photofit that bears little or no resemblance to the defendant should be admissible for the defence to show that the defendant is not the person who committed the crime. Since there are many more bad photofits than good, this is unlikely to be an attractive state of affairs, but is one that would inevitably follow if photofits were a special form of evidence in their own right.

The rule against hearsay covers not only the express contents of the prior statement, but also its implied assertions. In *Wright v Doe D Tatham* (1838), there was a dispute as to the mental capacity of the testator at the time he made his will. Letters written to the testator by various people were tendered to show he was sane. The court held that the letters were hearsay. If the writer had expressly stated that the testator was sane, the letters would be hearsay. Therefore the rule should also extend to implied assertions of sanity that could be made by looking at the contents of the letter.

This argument that the rule against hearsay extends to implied assertions was confirmed in *R v Kearley* (1992), although the Law Commission in their recent report recommended the admission of such evidence subject to a judicial warning about its weight.

2 Is the statement tendered to prove the truth of its contents?

The purpose for which the statement is tendered will determine whether the statement is hearsay or not. Only statements tendered as evidence of the truth of the matters contained in the statement will be hearsay.

The case of *R v Attard* (1958) illustrates the need to exercise care over the presentation of evidence to ensure that it does not fall foul of the rule against hearsay. A policeman gave evidence at trial of an interview he had conducted with a prisoner. Clearly this was a prior statement being tendered for the truth of contents, and so was hearsay. However, this would have been an exception to the rule, as it amounted to a confession by the prisoner. Unfortunately this would only be the case where the policeman knew what the prisoner had said. In *R v Attard*, the prisoner did not speak English, and so the policeman had no personal knowledge of what the prisoner said. The policeman could only recount what the interpreter said the prisoner had said. As such, what the interpreter said was a prior statement being tendered for the truth of its contents, and accordingly hearsay. The interpreter's remarks did not fall within any exception to the rule against hearsay, and were therefore inadmissible. Careful consideration by the prosecution could have avoided this difficulty by calling the interpreter to give evidence of what the prisoner said. Since the interpreter could understand the prisoner's comments he would be giving evidence of a confession by the prisoner that he had personally perceived being made, rather than one he had merely been told about, as was the case with the policeman.

In *Jones v Metcalfe* (1967) an avoidable mistake was again made. A witness had seen a crime and made a note of the registration number of the car that he had seen speeding away. This matched that of the defendant's car, although the defendant was denying any involvement with the offence. The witness had passed the information on to the police, who had failed to show him the note they made of his evidence, thereby removing any possibility of the witness using the police document to refresh his memory at trial. The witness did not keep his own note of the registration number, and at trial was unable to remember. The police note of the number was a prior statement, and since its only relevant purpose was the truth of its contents, it was hearsay and inadmissible.

Much of the rationale behind the rule against hearsay is to prevent evidence being admitted where the witness has not actually perceived the matters they are testifying or speaking about. Such evidence cannot safely be relied on as the witness does not know for a fact that the matter is true; they are relying on hearsay evidence.

This was applied in *Comptroller of Customs v Western Lectric* (1966) where a customs declaration as to the origin of goods was held to be hearsay. The declaration had been made by looking at the label on the goods, which amounts to a prior statement being tendered as proof of the truth of its contents. As any purchaser of fake designer goods knows, a Cartier label does not prove the watch was made by Cartier!

Likewise, in *R v Marshall* (1977), a defendant's statement that goods were stolen was inadmissible, since he did not know the goods were stolen, but had merely been told this by someone else. He was relying on the prior statement to establish the truth of the matters referred to, and this was hearsay.

Many of the most important pieces of information in our lives are actually hearsay evidence when properly examined. You do not know your date of birth; your birthday is hearsay evidence, as you have merely been told by others or by your birth certificate when you were born! Likewise most of us do not know as a fact who our parents are; we have merely been told this by others!

Statements tendered for some other relevant purpose

It is the reason for which a prior statement is tendered that renders it hearsay. If it is possible to demonstrate that a statement serves some relevant purpose other than proof of the truth of its contents then it will be admissible non-hearsay, original or circumstantial evidence.

Statements admissible as having a legal significance in their own right

In many cases it may be relevant to prove that a particular kind of statement was made, rather than needing to prove that its contents are true. Such statements have a legal significance in their own right. So, for example, in a breach of contract case W can give evidence that D said D would sell W a dog for £10. W is referring to a prior statement made by D, but not for the purpose of proving the truth of the statement, ie that D has a dog. Instead the statement is being referred to because it amounts to an offer, which is relevant to a breach of contract claim.

In defamation cases it is necessary to prove that a defamatory statement was published. Consequently when a sordid newspaper article is shown to the court, it is being tendered, not to prove the truth of its scurrilous accusations, but to show that the statement has been published, which is of relevance.

In *Subramaniam v The Public Prosecutor* (1956) the defendant was relying on a defence of duress in relation to a charge of illegal possession of firearms. The defendant wanted to give evidence of threats that had been made to him and his family, but the trial judge refused. This was wrong since the reference to the prior statements (the threats) was not being made to show that the threatening remarks were true, but merely to show that they had been made. The existence of threats is clearly relevant to a defence of duress.

Woodhouse v Hall (1981) is a famous illustration of this point. In that case an undercover policeman entered premises that were under suspicion of being a brothel. A woman who was employed on the premises offered to provide the policeman with sexual services, and at trial the policeman was allowed to repeat this statement. Although he was referring to the prior statement of the woman it was not for the purpose of proving the truth of what she said. Rather, it was to demonstrate that what she had said amounted to an offer of sexual services. This has a legal significance in relation to the offence of running a brothel, which can be committed by the provision or offering of sexual services. This offer by the identifiable woman who was employed on the premises was relevant as implicating the premises as a brothel. It can be further justified by pointing out that if the policeman is a reliable and truthful witness, then he has perceived the woman making the offer, and is giving direct evidence of the offer, and therefore his evidence is not hearsay.

Statements may also be relevant in their own right if they amount to acceptance, objections, or previous consistent or inconsistent statements which affect credibility, but which are not used to prove the truth of their contents.

Statements admissible to show the state of the mind of the maker

On many occasions it is relevant to establish the state of mind of a particular person. This can only ever be inferred from what the person does and says. Consequently prior statements may be admissible if they are tendered for the relevant purpose of establishing the state of mind of the maker of the remark.

The defendant in *Ratten v R* (1972) was accused of murdering his wife, and he argued that her shooting was an accident. The prosecution tendered evidence of a distraught phonecall made by the wife a few minutes before she was killed in which she asked for the police and was crying hysterically. The court felt that such evidence could serve a non-hearsay purpose. The prior statement by the wife demonstrated her terrified and frightened state of mind. Since she met her death a few minutes later at the hand of the defendant, a fact which was not denied, then her terrified state of mind was relevant in that it tended to suggest that accidental death was unlikely. Her state of mind demonstrated by her statement was circumstantial evidence that her death was deliberate.

The state of mind of the defendant must be relevant to an issue in the proceedings. In *R v Blastland* (1986) the defendant was accused of buggery and murder. He admitted the homosexual activities with the deceased victim before he died, but denied any involvement in the killing. As part of his defence he sought to admit statements made by another known homosexual, X, that had been made shortly after the victim had met with his death. X had apparently been very excited and distressed and had known of the murder, and the defence case was that this could implicate X and exonerate D. The House of Lords agreed that X's remarks were not hearsay, because they showed his excited and distressed state of mind. However, this was not relevant to the issue of whether D killed the victim, and was therefore inadmissible.

This issue of relevance to the issue in the proceedings formed the basis of the decisions in *R v Harry* (1988) and *R v Kearley* (1992). Both cases involved the police intercepting phonecalls made by unknown callers to the defendant's premises. In both cases the defendant was not present at the time, and the callers all asked to buy drugs, some mentioning the defendant by his name or nickname. It was held (by a majority in *R v Kearley*) that the statements by the callers were hearsay evidence if tendered to prove the truth of their implied assertions that the defendant had drugs, and that the premises were being used for the supply of drugs.

It could not be admitted as non-hearsay evidence either because, although the statements by the callers showed the state of mind of the callers, this was not relevant to the guilt of the defendant or the use of the premises. The case could be distinguished from *Woodhouse* in that, here, the calls were made by unknown individuals with no connection to the premises or the defendant. The calls implicated the callers and not the defendant. They were of no relevance to an offence of supplying drugs, which cannot be established by showing that unknown callers offered to buy drugs. The minority of the House of Lords thought that the calls could be circumstantial evidence as to the use of the premises.

R v Kearley and *R v Harry* may be understood by examining the following situations.

- If I am in a train station and walk past a beggar who asks me for money, this shows that the beggar hopes to get money from me. It does not tend to show that I have money, or that I would be prepared to give him any. It is no more relevant to the issue of my supplying money if I am asked by 10 beggars rather than one. They could all be labouring under the same mistake as to my generosity or financial state!

- Likewise if I am stopped in the street and asked if I have a light for a person's cigarette, this does not establish that I have matches or would be willing to supply them. If you substitute the request for money or matches with a request for drugs, then you have exactly the same situation as in *Kearley*.

In *R v Gilfoyle* (1996), the defendant was accused of murdering his wife who had been found hanged. The defence case was that she had committed suicide, and suicide notes were tendered as evidence of her relevant state of mind at the time. The prosecution called upon evidence, from some of the wife's friends, that she had told them that she was writing suicide notes at H's suggestion to help him with research. Whilst this would have been hearsay evidence if tendered to prove that she wrote the notes at H's suggestion, it was non-hearsay evidence of the wife's state of mind. Far from being suicidal, the conversations showed she regarded the situation as a joke, and was not unhappy.

Sometimes a prior statement is tendered because it is argued that the statement is false, and that this falsity demonstrates the guilty state of mind of the maker of the statement. In *R v Mawaz and Amasat Khan*

(1967) the two defendants had given identical alibis when accused of murder. The prosecution argued that if the jury viewed the alibis to be untrue then this could be evidence incriminating both defendants. This was upheld as the statements had a relevance in tending to show that the men were acting together to give the same false alibi, which indicated a common guilt.

Statements relevant to indicate the state of mind of the perceiver

A prior statement may be tendered in evidence to show the effect of the statement on the person who perceived the statement being made. In *Subramaniam v The Public Prosecutor* (1956) the threats were admissible to show the effect they had on the defendant's state of mind. This was relevant to whether his free will had been overcome for duress to be established.

Statements with relevance because of the circumstances in which they were found

It is possible to make reference to a prior statement and argue that there is a circumstantial relevance through the fact that the statement was found in a particular place or circumstances.

In *R v Rice and Others* (1963) the defendant was accused with others of being a party to a conspiracy, and it was part of the prosecution case that the defendant had flown to Manchester on a particular date with another accused. The prosecution tendered two used airline tickets that had been recovered from an airline in the name of the defendant and co-accused for a flight to Manchester on the day in question. The defence argued that the tickets were hearsay, and this would have been the case if they had been tendered merely for the truth of their contents. However, the fact that the ticket was recovered from the airline, given the airline's procedures for ticketing, check in and boarding, meant it was a commonsense inference that two people using those names had taken the flight in question. This was circumstantial evidence from which the jury might infer that the persons in question were the defendant and co-accused. *Rice* has been subject to a great deal of criticism, but it is not the only case to draw circumstantial inferences from where the document was found.

In *R v Lydon* (1986) the defendant was accused of robbery, in respect of which he raised an alibi defence. Along the route taken by the robber a gun was found, similar to that used in the robbery, as well as some scraps of paper with the name Sean on them. The defendant's name was Sean, and the ink on the paper matched ink on the barrel of the gun. The defence argued that the paper was inadmissible hearsay, but the Court of Appeal held that it was not. There was no way that the paper could be tendered for the truth of its contents, nor could the contents impliedly assert the defendant was the robber. Instead the relevance of the paper was its link to the gun and getaway route, and the circumstantial inference that the defendant was involved because of the circumstances in which the paper was found.

More recently, in *Roberts v DPP* (1994) the defendant denied being involved in the running of premises that were used as a brothel. Various bills and correspondence relating to the premises were found in the defendant's possession. The finding of the bills in such circumstances was relevant in that it tended to show that the defendant was involved, or else why would he have the bills?

Statements that are relevant because of absence of record

Statements that positively assert a fact are hearsay if tendered as proof of the truth of the fact. Likewise statements that are negative in their effect, which point to a particular fact not existing or having occurred may be negative hearsay.

In *R v Patel* (1981) the defendant was accused of being an illegal immigrant. The prosecution sought to establish this by calling an immigration official to testify that there was no record of the defendant being granted permission to enter the UK. The court held that this was hearsay evidence, even though the absence of the record was in a negative form. However, there was *dicta* in *Patel* that such evidence could be admissible if the right official with responsibility for the records testified as to the absence of an entry in the records. The absence of a record could then arguably be regarded as circumstantial evidence.

This was explored in *R v Shone* (1983) where the defendant was accused of handling stolen motor parts. The parts were recorded in the company records, which were then added to if the parts were used in repairs or sold. There was no indication that the parts in question had been used or sold, and since they were not in stock the court was prepared to draw the inference that they had been stolen. In *Shone* the persons responsible for the compilation of the records testified, and so the absence of the record was circumstantial evidence that the goods were stolen.

Mechanical calculations by machines and computers

Increasingly, technology makes it possible for machines and computers to be used to provide information. The status of the information will be hearsay if it involves human input or discretion, but will be real evidence if the machine or computer has performed a mechanical calculation without human input or interference. In *R v Woods* (1982) it was argued that a device that merely performs a calculation that could have been done manually and which involves no knowledge or discretion from the device produces real, not hearsay evidence.

This means that readings from a speedometer, police radar gun, intoximeter, calculator and other such device will not be subject to the rule against hearsay. However, such evidence will require the court to be satisfied that the device was working properly.

In *R v Spiby* (1991) a telephone exchange automatically logged calls, and charged hotel guests for the call depending on where the call was made to and how long it lasted. Since there was never any human involvement in the recording of the information the evidence generated was held to be real evidence.

10 The common law exceptions

Introduction

The rule against hearsay developed through fear of the unreliability of hearsay evidence. However, the common law recognised that, in certain circumstances, evidence that was technically hearsay should be admissible. There was no general exception allowing hearsay to be admitted on the basis of its reliability, rather, the common law developed piecemeal exceptions which have reliability as their basis.

The *res gestae*

Hearsay that forms part of the *res gestae* may be admissible. The *res gestae* exception covers remarks made by participants and observers of events in circumstances where the remark is so bound up in the event that it can be safely admitted. In the USA this is termed the 'excited utterances' rule and renders admissible spontaneous and uncalculated remarks that can be safely relied on as truthful. This is because the event is such that it has dominated the mind of the maker in such a way that the maker is unlikely to fabricate or distort his account.

The statement must be bound up with the act or event in order to form part of the *res gestae* (*R v Bliss* (1837)), where a casual remark about the planting of a tree on a boundary was inadmissible as it was not so bound up in the act to be part of the event.

The statement must be spontaneous or contemporaneous to the event in order to be admissible. In *Thompson v Trevanion* (1693) a wife's remarks on being assaulted by her husband were admissible if made immediately, since she would not have had time to think about what to say, and give an account that was unduly favourable to her or damaging to her husband.

The requirement of spontaneity was misapplied in *R v Bedingfield* (1879), a case which was later overruled. In this case the victim of a terrible attack stumbled from the room where the attack had taken place. Although her throat was slit she managed to utter remarks identifying the defendant as her attacker. These remarks were inadmissible since the event to which she was referring was deemed to have ended and the remarks were therefore not viewed as sufficiently spontaneous.

In *Ratten v R* (1972) the hysterical phonecall from the victim was held to be non-hearsay circumstantial evidence. However, the Privy Council thought that, if it had been hearsay, it would have been a *res gestae* remark. *R v Bedingfield* was subjected to severe criticism, as having missed the point of the *res gestae* exception. Admissibility did not depend upon a strict test of time, but on whether:

... the statement was so made in circumstances of spontaneity or involvement in the event that the possibility of concoction can be disregarded ... the utterance can be safely regarded as a true reflection of what was unrolling or actually happening.

Thus it is a question of whether the possibility of fabrication or concoction existed, something that was emphasised by the House of Lords in *R v Andrews* (1987). In this case the stabbed victim of a robbery lapsed into a coma and died two months later. Before he was rushed to hospital, he made remarks to a policeman identifying his attackers, but the remark could not be admitted as a dying declaration, since he did not believe he was about to die. The trial judge admitted the statement as part of the *res gestae* and this was upheld by the House of Lords. The real test in such cases is whether there is 'no real opportunity for reasoned reflection' and that 'the mind of the declarant was still dominated by the event'.

In *Andrews* it was thought that ordinarily the prospect of the witness being mistaken should affect the weight to be given to the statement but, in special cases, the possibility of error could affect admissibility, for example extreme intoxication or blindness. Likewise, if there was a suggestion that the witness bore the defendant any malice, then this would have to be borne in mind in determining whether there was the opportunity for concoction. In *Andrews* it was also suggested that the *res gestae* rule should not be used where the witness who made the remark was available to testify, but had not been called to do so.

It is useful to contrast *R v Nye and Loan* (1977) with *Tobi v Nicholas* (1988). In *Nye* the victim had been involved in a car crash, and had then been assaulted by the occupants of the other car. He had received blows to the head, and when the police arrived some 15 minutes later he told then what happened and identified his attackers. Although he had responded to the police question, the remark was still the *res gestae*. The event had been very traumatic for the victim, who had been trying to recover from the blows when the police arrived. The victim in *Nye* also testified, which ensured that the defence could have explored any doubts about his credibility, motive or error. In *Tobi v Nicholas* the driver of a coach which had been involved in a collision volunteered to go with the police to the defendant's house and, on seeing the defendant, the coach driver accused him of causing the collision. The prosecution did not call the coach driver to give evidence and instead tried to rely on the *res gestae* to allow a police officer to recount what the coach driver had said at the defendant's house. This was held to be inadmissible as the collision had not been so traumatic that the coach driver could be regarded as making comments while the event still dominated his mind, thus removing the possibility of concoction.

Statements referring to the physical state of the maker

It is possible to admit a prior statement as proof of the truth of its contents when the maker of the prior statement refers to how they feel, or to their physical condition at that time. In *R v Conde* (1868) a child made complaints of being hungry to a neighbour. This was admissible to show that the child was hungry and starving just before it died.
Although the statement is admissible to show the contemporaneous state of the maker at the time the remark was made, the statement is inadmissible in so far as it refers to a possible cause of the physical state.

In *Re Gloster* (1888) a woman was dying as a result of an illegal abortion, and she named the defendant as the person who had performed the operation. Whilst the statement would have been admissible to show the woman's state at that time, it was inadmissible to show the cause. Such a statement would only be admissible as a dying declaration.

Statements by persons now deceased

If the maker of certain types of statements has died, and is therefore unable to repeat the statement in court, then the statement may be admissible at common law. This exception does not apply to all statements made by persons who have subsequently died, only those that fall within the following narrow categories

- Matters of public concern
  If the statement by the deceased related to a matter of public concern, or the existence of public rights, then the statement will be admissible at common law. The statement needs to have been made before litigation was contemplated, and must be directly relevant to the existence of the right.
- Statements relating to family pedigree
  A statement by a person now deceased that related directly to family pedigree and which was made before litigation was contemplated is another antiquated common law exception used to help establish legitimacy, validity of marriage, succession, etc.
- Declarations against financial or proprietary interest
  In *Higham v Ridgeway* (1808), a deceased midwife had attended a birth and stated that he had been paid for his services in delivering that child on that particular date. This statement was admissible since it went against the midwife's financial interest to admit that he was no longer owed money. His statement was then admitted as proof of the truth of its contents, and could therefore be used to establish the birth of the particular child in question.
  Thus the statement must be one that the maker realises is against his financial or proprietary interest, and this does not cover other forms of incriminating statements, even though they may show possible penal consequences.
  In *R v Rogers* (1994) the deceased had told his wife that some men were after him for money for some drugs, and that the drugs were for him and that the accused who was on trial knew nothing about the large quantities of heroin involved, or the firearms on the premises. This was inadmissible, as there was no declaration against financial or proprietary interest, since the deceased was not acknowledging that he owed the money. Therefore this could not be used by the accused to excuse himself.
- Declarations in the course of duty
  Statements made by the deceased that are in the course of his legal, professional, or possibly moral, duties are admissible to prove the

truth of the facts stated by the deceased. The statement must refer to what the deceased was doing and had personal knowledge of, and must be contemporaneous to the event it refers to, ie as soon as practicable.

This was used in *R v Buckley* (1873) to admit statements by a policeman to his superior officer that the policeman was going to see the defendant. The deceased police officer was found dead shortly after, and his statement was used to incriminate the defendant in his murder. The statement was made showing what the deceased was doing at the time in question, and he had a duty to do that thing and to make the report or record.

If there is no duty to make the record or report, then the statement is inadmissible. Contrast two cases involving surveyor's records: *Mercer v Denne* (1905) where the duty did not require the making of the record and was inadmissible, with *Mellor v Walmesley* (1905) where the duty did involve the records being kept, which were accordingly admissible.

Only statements of fact are admissible under this exception: *R v McGuire* (1985), where a report by a forensic scientist containing his opinion on the cause of a fire was inadmissible after his death.

• Dying declarations

In homicide cases where causing death forms part of the offence, then the dying declaration of the victim as to the cause of his death is admissible. This is not available if the death does not form part of the offence that the defendant is charged with: *R v Hind* (1860), where the dying declaration of a woman was inadmissible in a case where the defendant was charged with procuring her miscarriage.

This is justified in the interest of justice to ensure that the defendant has to answer to the accusation of the deceased that the defendant caused the death (*R v Nembhard* (1981)), and also on the basis that statements made just before death are likely to be reliable (*R v Woodcock* (1789)). In *Woodcock* it was stated that persons with a 'settled hopeless expectation of death' are unlikely to lie at such a stage in their life.

It is necessary to look at the state of mind of the maker of the statement to see whether they actually had a belief in their impending death. The maker must give up all hope of recovery (*R v Errington* (1838)) and it is irrelevant whether those around, such as the medical staff, also share this belief (*R v Peel* (1860)). In *Peel* the deceased thought he was going to die, whereas the doctor treating him was optimistic that he would recover.

Courts are likely to infer an expectation of death where the deceased shows an awareness of the severity of his condition, and this may be strengthened or weakened by the other actions of the deceased. In *R v Spilsbury* (1835) the deceased did not make any farewell gestures to his wife, nor try to organise his affairs or give instructions for his funeral. This tended to suggest that he did not believe he was about to die.

The impending death need not be immediately expected; it will be enough that the deceased expected to die within a short time of making the statement (*R v Austin* (1912)), even though he may actually die much later, as in *R v Bernadotti* (1869), where death resulted some three weeks after the dying declaration.

This understanding of the imminence of death makes it difficult for a young child to make a dying declaration, since they do not usually have the level of understanding necessary: *R v Pike* (1829), where the declaration of a child of four was inadmissible.

The dying declaration must have been completed by the deceased since, if he fails to finish what he was saying, there is no accurate picture being presented, as in *Waugh v The King* (1950), where the victim lapsed into a coma in the middle of his statement.

A valid dying declaration will be left to the jury to evaluate, although it is good practice for the judge to remind them that the statement has not been tested by cross-examination, and to exercise care: *R v Nembhard* (1981).

Public documents

If a document has been compiled for public record by someone acting in the course of a public duty or office, then the document is admissible as proof of the truth of its contents as an exception to the rule against hearsay. The document has to be one that the public have access to, and are entitled to inspect, and this would cover documents such as the register of births, marriages and deaths.

Many such documents would also be admissible under the wider statutory provisions of s 24 Criminal Justice Act 1988.

Admissions

An admission is a statement wholly or partly adverse to the maker, at both common law and by virtue of s 82 PACE 1984. The detrimental nature of such a statement is thought to give it reliability, and that is why hearsay statements that amount to confessions are admissible. This can cover statements made orally, in writing or any other way such as a gesture.

The common law rules on admissions, or confessions, as they are termed in criminal cases, has been supplemented by statutory provisions in PACE 1984, and it is possible to have a valid confession according to common law principles that is nevertheless inadmissible because it falls foul of the provisions in ss 76 or 78 PACE 1984. These statutory provisions are discussed in more detail in later chapters.

The general rule

Normally an admission or confession only incriminates the maker, and not anyone else mentioned in the statement. Therefore an admission is only admissible as an exception to the rule against hearsay in respect of the maker. The jury will be told that the confession is not admissible evidence against anyone else, since it is hearsay evidence: *R v Rhodes* (1959).

The confession will only be admissible if the defendant knows what he is talking about, since confessions based on hearsay must themselves be excluded: *Comptroller of Customs v Western Lectric* (1966), where declarations regarding the origin of goods was inadmissible since it was based on a label and not actual knowledge of the goods' origin.

It is possible that extensive experience will give rise to knowledge, as in *R v Chatwood* (1980), where an experienced drug user confessed to possessing drugs, and this sufficed even though there was no expert evidence available to him.

Confessions binding persons other than the maker

* Statements in the course of the common design
  In *R v Blake and Tye* (1844), the defendants were accused of a conspiracy to evade customs duty. The documents that had been drawn up by D1 to further this common design and help achieve their

criminal objective were admissible against D1, the maker, and also against D2, who was a party to the common design. However, documentary records on D1's chequebook, which were for his own purposes, were admissible only against D1, since they were not in pursuit of the common design, and had been made after the common design had ended. Statements made to the police by D1 after arrest will not be admissible against D2 since this will be outside the common design: *R v Walters* (1979).

The existence of a common design between D1 and D2 must be proved by separate independent evidence, and not just the statement of a co-conspirator: *R v Governor of Pentonville Prison, ex p Osman* (1990).

- Agency

  The admission of an agent will bind the principal, provided that the agent acts within the scope of his agency. This can arise where a lawyer makes admissions on behalf of a client when acting on the client's instructions, and can arise in other circumstances, although note there is no automatic agency between spouses.

- Silence

  In certain circumstances silence by the accused can amount to an admission of the truth of allegations made in his presence by another.

  Where the accusations are made by an ordinary person then, if they are on equal footing with the defendant, and it would be reasonable to expect a reply to the accusation, then the defendant's silence can amount to an acceptance of the truth of the accusation, and the defendant will be bound by the statement: *R v Mitchell* (1892). In this case a dying woman made accusations about the defendant on her deathbed in the presence of the defendant. The defendant did not challenge the remarks, but the judge held that this was not an acceptance. It was hardly reasonable to expect the defendant to argue with the woman as she lay dying.

  In *R v Parkes* (1976) the defendant was accused of murder. When the victim's mother found her injured, the mother went to the defendant and accused him of being responsible. He did not respond to the allegation, and when the woman threatened to call the police she was stabbed by the defendant. The totality of the defendant's response indicated an acceptance of the accusations, but arguably his silence alone would have sufficed, although it clearly would not have been so weighty.

  Where the silence is in the face of accusations by the police or other persons in authority, the position is different. Technically the accused has a right to silence, and the traditional view is that silence in the face of police accusations does not amount to an acceptance: *R v Hall* (1971). The police and suspect are not on equal footing, but there was a suggestion in *R v Chandler* (1976) that the jury could be invited to draw adverse inferences from a defendant's silence when an accusation was made in the presence of the defendant's solicitor. *Chandler* was a case where the accusation was made before the accused had been cautioned, and arguably will not apply where a suspect has been cautioned, and told of his right to remain silent.

This right to remain silent without adverse inferences being drawn has been severely restricted by ss 34, 36 and 37 of the Criminal Justice and Public Order Act 1994, which are discussed in more detail later. Section 34 allows adverse inferences to be drawn from a defendant's failure to raise issues that he subsequently relies on at trial. Sections 36 and 37 deal with the defendant's failure to explain various damaging matters such as possession of incriminating articles or presence in an incriminating location.

11 Statutory exceptions in criminal law

The Criminal Justice Act 1988

Sections 23 and 24 CJA 1988 admit documentary hearsay in certain circumstances in criminal cases, and have made dramatic and more extensive allowances than the common law.

Section 23 CJA 1988

Admissibility under s 23(1)

Section 23 has the effect of admitting first hand documentary hearsay. Section 23(1) provides:

A statement made by a person in a document shall be admissible in criminal proceedings as evidence of any fact of which direct oral evidence by him would be admissible.

It is necessary to look at the component parts of this subsection in more detail and to analyse whether they are satisfied by the facts of any given case.

- 'Statement' is defined by reference to the Civil Evidence Act 1968, Sched 2 CJA 1988, and means any representation of fact, whether by words or otherwise.

113

- 'Document' is given an inclusive definition, and includes maps, plans, drawings, graphs, photographs, discs, tapes, sound tracks or other devices by which sound may be recorded, films, negatives, tapes or other device by which visual images may be produced (Sched 2 CJA 1988). Consequently any tangible method of recording information would seem to fall within the definition of document.

- 'Made by a person in a document' requires the person making the statement to check that a document has been made and that it is accurate if the document is drawn up by someone other than the maker of the statement. In *R v McGillivray* (1993) the victim had been very badly burned in an attack and had made a statement to a policeman in the presence of a nurse. The victim was too ill to sign the statement, but the policeman read it back to the victim who agreed its contents. This was held to be a statement made in a document.

  It would seem to follow that the civil case of *Ventouris v Mountain (No 2)* (1992) would apply to the interpretation of this provision, whereby a secret recording, made without the maker's knowledge, of his remarks would not qualify as a statement made in a document.

- 'Admissible as evidence of any fact' means that the prior statement under s 23 is admissible as proof of the matters stated therein, although the evidence is still hearsay.

- '... of which direct oral evidence by him [the maker] would be admissible' requires the maker of the statement to be recounting events or facts that he has perceived, rather than merely repeating hearsay accounts, and for such an account to be otherwise admissible. Implied in this is a requirement that the maker of the statement would have been competent to testify at trial, and if there is a doubt about their mental capacity to do so, then s 23 will not be satisfied: *R v Irish* (1994). In *Irish* the prosecution tendered a statement by a confused and senile old man who had been the victim of a fraud. The court excluded the statement under s 23, but it is submitted that the case was wrongly decided. The statement was not actually being tendered as proof of the truth of its contents, rather it was to show the confused state of mind of the victim, which was relevant to how he was conned by the defendant. The evidence should never have been classified as hearsay, it was relevant non-hearsay evidence of the maker's state of mind, and s 23 did not therefore need to be satisfied.

Reason for non-attendance

It is then necessary to establish that the maker of the statement will not testify for one of the reasons specified in s 23(2) or s 23(3). The party wishing to use the statement has the burden of proving admissibility, and therefore it is necessary to bring forward evidence at trial to establish the s 23 reason. If the prosecution is seeking to use the section they must prove admissibility beyond reasonable doubt (*R v Acton Justices ex p McMullen* (1991)), whereas the defence merely have to prove on the balance of probabilities (*R v Mattey* (1995)).

In *R v Case* (1991) the prosecution merely tendered statements made by the victims of a crime who lived overseas. The fact that they lived overseas was apparent from the statement, and since no extra evidence was produced to prove that the witnesses were outside the UK and that it was not reasonably practicable for them to attend the statement should not have been admitted. Further the reason must be properly established without resorting to inadmissible hearsay: *Neill v N Antrim Magistrates* (1992), where a policeman's evidence that a child witness was in fear was inadmissible since the policeman had not interviewed the child, but had merely relied on the mother telling him of the fear.

- 'The person who made the statement is dead or by reason of his bodily or mental condition unfit to attend as a witness': s 23(2)(a)

  It clearly is not possible to call someone to testify if they have died since making the statement, and s 23 also makes allowances for those who are unfit physically or mentally to testify. In *R v Setz Dempsey* (1994) this was held to include a witness suffering from a mental condition that caused them extreme anxiety when under stress.

- 'The person who made the statement is outside the UK and it is not reasonably practicable to secure his attendance': s 23(2)(b).

  This reason requires the establishing of the physical presence of the witness outside the UK. This is a physical, geographical requirement, and does not turn on diplomatic niceties: *R v Jiminez Paez* (1994), where it was unsuccessfully argued that a Colombian embassy official in London was outside the UK because of his presence in the embassy!

  There is then the additional requirement of it not being reasonably practicable to secure attendance. This does not merely mean on the morning of the trial; all the circumstances of the case, and the measures that can ordinarily be taken to secure attendance must be considered. In *R v Bray* (1988), a case decided under a similar provision in earlier legislation, the prosecution only realised on the morning of the trial that the witness had been in South Korea for the past seven months. Since they had taken no steps to secure attendance the requirement was not satisfied. Contrast this with *R v French* (1993), where the prosecution had made a number of unsuccessful attempts to secure attendance.

In *R v Castillo* (1996), the court indicated that in considering whether it would be practicable for the witness to attend, the importance of the witness' evidence, together with the expense and inconvenience involved, should be considered.

- 'All reasonable steps have been taken to find the person who made the statement, but that he cannot be found': s 23(2)(c).

  It will be necessary to provide evidence to the court of the steps that had been taken to find the witness. This could include enquiries to the police, social security and passport agencies.

- 'The statement was made to a police officer or some other person charged with the duty of investigating offences or charging offenders and the person does not give oral evidence through fear or because he is kept out of the way': s 23(3).

  Fear must be a genuine fear, as in *R v O'Loughlin* (1988), where threats and intimidation in a terrorist case would suffice. However, there is no need for the fear to be objectively reasonable (*R v Acton Justices ex p McMullen* (1991)), provided that 'the witness is in fear as a consequence of the commission of the material offence or of something said or done subsequently in relation to that offence and the possibility of the witness testifying as to it'. Thus, the fear must arise because of the present proceedings, an earlier bad experience in relation to other proceedings of the witness or someone he knows will not suffice.

  There is no mention in the section, which has been criticised by many as creating more problems of interpretation than necessary, as to who has to be responsible for creating the fear. In most cases this will be attributable to defence actions, but if the fear arises as a consequence of prosecution actions, then it would be wrong to allow the prosecution to use the statement, which would be excluded under s 78 PACE 1984.

  In *Neill v N Antrim Magistrates* (1992) this section was used by the prosecution to try to admit statements by two boys detailing an assault and identifying their attackers. The statement was held to be inadmissible because there was no admissible evidence of the fear, only a hearsay account relayed to the police by the mother.

  This section operates where the witness is unable to attend court to testify through fear, but it also applies where a witness begins to testify but cannot continue through fear: *R v Ashford Magistrates ex p Hilden* (1993). It was agreed that this would cover the witness who had given no significantly relevant evidence up to the point of being unable to continue, but Popplewell J went further and thought that it could apply regardless of at what point the witness feels unable to continue.

Being kept away will usually arise where the defendant or his associates have taken actions to keep the witness away from court, but again the requirement may be satisfied if the prosecution are responsible for keeping the witness away.

If the statement satisfies the requirements of s 23, it will be necessary to consider whether it will be excluded. The discretion to admit and exclude evidence under ss 25 and 26 CJA will be considered later with other exclusionary discretions.

Section 24 CJA 1988

Admissibility under s 24(1)

Section 24 allows the use of documentary hearsay in circumstances where the document was created in a sufficiently formal situation, relating to trade or business documents, and where the supplier of the information had personal knowledge of the facts they were passing on. As such s 24 is capable of applying to secondhand hearsay.

Section 24(1) provides:

A statement in a document shall be admissible in criminal proceedings as evidence of any fact of which direct oral evidence would be admissible if ...

(i)   the document was created or received by a person in the course of a trade, business, profession or other occupation, or as the holder of a paid or unpaid office; and

(ii)   the information contained in the document was supplied by a person (whether or not the maker of the statement) who had, or may reasonably be supposed to have had personal knowledge of the matters dealt with.

- 'Statement' and 'document' mean the same here as in s 23, but there is no requirement that the statement be made in the document. Therefore the section could apply where the maker of the statement does not realise that a document has been created, or where he has not checked its accuracy.
- 'Of which direct oral evidence would be admissible' serves, as it did in s 23, to ensure that evidence is only admissible if the original maker of the statement would have been a competent witness at the

time he made the statement, and that the statement does not contain remarks that infringe any other rules on admissibility.

- 'Created or received in the course of trade, business, profession ... occupation, ... or paid or unpaid office.' This wide definition of the type of document admissible will cover a variety of documents created or received in circumstances that should give rise to a certain degree of reliability. It has applied to police documents, liquidator's documents, bank records and doctor's records.

- '... supplied by a person ... who had, or may be reasonably supposed to have had, personal knowledge of the matters dealt with.' The requirement of personal knowledge on the part of the supplier of the information should operate to ensure reliability of the documentary hearsay. It is not clear when personal knowledge can be implied. This may arguably be difficult if the supplier is an unknown individual, and the basis of his knowledge cannot be safely assumed because the information is not supplied in circumstances where knowledge can be inferred. This would emphasise the difference between a statement made by an unknown eyewitness at the scene of a crime, with that of an unknown phonecaller leaving a message some time after the offence. In the first it will be easy to establish the necessary personal knowledge, whereas in the second there will be difficulty.

Section 24(2) provides that if the information was received indirectly then:

'each person through whom it was supplied received it in the course of a trade, business, profession, occupation, paid or unpaid office.'

Thus in a multiple hearsay case, every intermediary who does not have personal knowledge must receive the information in their business, trade, etc capacity. Oddly, there is no requirement that they pass the information on in that capacity.

Reasons for non-attendance

If a document satisfies the requirements of s 24(1) and s 24(2) then it will be admissible in its own right, and will stand as evidence of the facts stated therein. However, if the statement was prepared for the purpose of criminal investigation or criminal proceedings then the additional requirement of s 24(4) must be satisfied, and a reason for non-attendance be established.

Section 24(4) reasons for non-attendance include the s 23(2) and s 23(3) reasons discussed earlier, but also the additional reason in s 24(4)(iii) which states:

The person who made the statement cannot reasonably be expected (having regard to the time that has elapsed since he made the statement and to all the circumstances) to have any recollection of the matters dealt with in the statement.

It is not terribly clear who this requirement refers to: the original eye witness who made the statement, or the person who made the statement in the document when they compiled the document. The original intention of Parliament was for it to be the eye witness since, clearly, if they could remember then it would be preferable to have their oral account of events instead of the document. However, the wording of the section is open to another interpretation, and there are cases where a more literal interpretation has been used by the courts, resulting in the application of s 24(4)(iii) to the compiler of the statement in the document.

In *R v Bedi* (1992), bank documents compiled from reports of stolen credit cards were held to be outside s 24(4) since they were compiled for the bank's own purposes and not for criminal investigations. However, if the document had been within s 24(4) then it was assumed that it would be the bank clerk to whom the section applied, not the owners of cards who made the original report.

This was also used in *R v Carrington* (1994), where an eye witness noted the registration number of a car she had seen leaving the scene of a crime. The eyewitness reported this to her supervisor, who made a record of the number. At trial the eye witness could not remember the number, nor did she have her original note available as a memory refreshing document since it had been destroyed. However, the supervisor's record was admitted under s 24, and it was held that the supervisor could not be reasonably expected to have recollection of the matters. This can be criticised in that the maker of the statement in the document will usually never have any independent knowledge of the matters anyway, at best they can only recollect what they have been told. As such the document is at best a memory refreshing document as to what they were told; it should not be admissible hearsay under s 24. Perhaps this difficulty can be circumvented by seeking to exclude such documents where there is doubt about the fairness of admitting them.

Evidence that satisfies the requirements of s 24 must then be judged according to the discretions to admit and exclude evidence in ss 25 and 26 of CJA 1988.

Exclusion of evidence under the CJA

Section 25

Section 25 gives the judge a discretion to exclude evidence that would otherwise be admissible under s 23 or s 24. This discretion is to be exercised if it would not be in the interests of justice to admit the evidence: s 25(1).

Section 25(2) specifies factors that the court should take into account in addition to all the circumstances of the case:

* 'the nature and source of the document ... and to whether or not ... it is likely that the document is authentic';
* 'the extent to which the statement appears to supply evidence which would not otherwise be readily available';
* 'the relevance of the evidence ... to any issue in the proceedings';
* 'to any risk, having regard in particular to whether it is likely to be possible to controvert the statement if the person making it does not attend to give oral evidence in the proceedings, that its admission or exclusion will result in unfairness to the accused'.

The emphasis of this section is on admitting the evidence unless the interests of justice require exclusion (*R v Cole* (1990)), and the burden of proof is on the person wanting to exclude the evidence.

Section 26

However, if the document has been prepared for the purpose of criminal proceedings or investigations then s 26 applies. This provides:

> The statement shall not be given in evidence ... without leave of the court, and the court shall not give leave unless it is of the opinion that the statement ought to be admitted in the interests of justice.

According to *R v Cole* the emphasis in s 26 is on excluding such statements and the burden of proof is on the person seeking to admit the statement. Whilst s 26 applies to statements prepared for criminal proceedings or investigations, s 25 is not limited to any particular kind of statement. Therefore statements under s 26, could technically also be considered under s 25, although this is probably unnecessary: *R v Grafton* (1995). However, it would be a mistake to only apply s 25 to such statements: *R v Setz-Dempsey* (1994).

Section 26 directs the court to have regard to:

(i)   the contents of the statement;
(ii) the risk ... that its admission or exclusion will result in unfairness to the accused (same as s 25(2)(d));
(iii) any other circumstances that appear to the court to be relevant.

Important considerations

In determining what way the discretion will be exercised it may be useful to consider the following matters.

The contents of the statement

In *R v Patel* (1993) the court had to consider the admissibility of a witness statement by a witness providing very weak alibi evidence for the defence. The very basic nature of the statement and the fact that the statement could therefore have been discredited by cross-examination were factors that influenced the court to exclude the evidence.

If weak statements are admitted, or if they are flawed by inconsistency or some other factor such as drunkenness, then the judge must point out the weaknesses in the evidence to the jury: *R v Kennedy* (1994). *Kennedy* was considered to be a borderline case by the Court of Appeal where the judge's decision to admit the statement by a drunken inconsistent witness who had died was upheld, but his failure to warn of the weaknesses was criticised.

In *R v Patel* the court did not feel that the argument that the more crucial the evidence the more likely it should be excluded was justified. In fact it is often in the interests of justice to admit strong crucial evidence, although the courts are wary of admitting a statement that forms the principle part of the prosecution case in documentary form. This is because it would be wrong to convict the defendant on the basis of one uncontroverted piece of evidence: *Neill v N Antrim Magistrates' Court* (1992).

There is a reluctance to admit identification evidence by document (*Neill v N Antrim Magistrates' Court*) since such evidence is often inherently unreliable (*R v Turnbull* (1977)) in a manner that only really becomes apparent on cross-examination (*R v Setz Dempsey* (1994)). There is a greater willingness to admit accounts of what happened rather than accounts of identification or recognition.

Risk of unfairness through inability to controvert

The mere fact that the evidence cannot be the subject of cross-examination does not justify exclusion. However, the judge must consider how far it will be possible to controvert the evidence. This may be achieved by having the opportunity to cross-examine other prosecution witnesses, but it is not limited to this. Thus, if the defendant has the opportunity to controvert the evidence by testifying himself, or by calling his own witnesses, then this may mitigate the injustice to him. In *R v Cole* (1990) the statement by a witness who had died before trial was admitted because there were other prosecution witnesses available who could be cross-examined about their accounts, and the defence could also call their own witnesses to support their case of self-defence. The defendant could also have testified to give his account of the incident, thus contradicting the version given by the deceased witness.

There is no rule that says a statement is inadmissible if the only way of controverting it is by the defendant testifying: *R v Price* (1991), where a bank manager's note of a meeting was admissible and not excluded under s 25, even though the only way of controverting the manager's account would have been by the defendant testifying.

Identification evidence is difficult to controvert if in a document: *Neill v N Antrim Magistrates' Court* (1992).

Sometimes the difficulty of controverting the evidence can be overcome by giving advance notice to the opponent of the intention to use the hearsay statement, as in *R v Iqbal* (1990), where the prosecution had six months to investigate the reliability of the hearsay statement.

Other circumstances

The courts can look at a wide range of other circumstances of the case in order to determine what would be in the interests of justice. It is likely that evidence would be excluded if the reason for the non-availability of the witness is the fault of the prosecution, as in *R v French* (1993). Conversely the prosecution are more likely to be able to use statements where they can demonstrate that the reason for non-attendance is due to the act of the defendant in putting the witness in fear. Greater willingness to admit evidence is also demonstrated where the witness is dead, rather than for another less dramatic reason, such as the witness being away on a round the world cruise!

Other discretions to exclude

Sections 25 and 26 do not remove the discretion to exclude evidence that is admissible under s 23 or s 24 by reference to other powers of the court. Thus s 28(1)(b) preserves the discretion to exclude under s 78 PACE 1984 on the basis that the admission of prosecution evidence would adversely affect the fairness of proceedings, and the *R v Sang* (1980) discretion to exclude on the basis that the prejudicial effect of the prosecution evidence outweighs the probative value. Neither of these discretions allows the exclusion of defence evidence, and it is difficult to see how they add anything to the discretions in ss 25 or 26 in relation to prosecution evidence.

Schedule 2 CJA 1988

Schedule 2 of the Act contains certain supplementary provisions. In para 1 provision is made for the credibility of the maker of the statement to be attacked, and this can be done, for example, by using previous inconsistent statements by the maker. This occurred in the trial of Rose West, where the statement by her dead husband that he alone and was responsible for the murders of which she stood accused was admitted for the defence under s 23. This then opened the door for the prosecution to prove various previous inconsistent statements by him where he admitted acting with others and had said he was covering up for someone. Th se statements were not admissible to prove the truth of their contents,   ' were admissible to attack Fred West's credibility as the maker of the hearsay statement admissible under s 23.

Paragraph 2 provides that s 23 or s 24 statements do not amount to corroboration of the maker's evidence.

Paragraph 3 provides that the weight to be given to the evidence depends on all the circumstances of the case and what inferences can be reasonably drawn.

Other miscellaneous statutory exceptions to the rule against hearsay

The Criminal Justice and Public Order Act 1994 abolishes the following statutory exceptions.

- Criminal Justice Act 1925 s 13(3)
  This allowed the use of depositions that had been taken before examining justices if the witness was later unable to attend because they were dead, insane, too ill to travel, or kept out of the way by the accused. There was a discretion to exclude such evidence.
- Magistrates' Courts Act 1980 s 102
  This extends s 13(3) above to evidence in a deposition taken in committal proceedings.
- MCA 1980 s 103
  Permits the use of statements of child witnesses under 14 in certain offences for committal purposes only.
- MCA 1980 s 105
  Permits the use of depositions from those dangerously ill provided the opportunity to cross-examine has been provided.
- Children and Young Persons Act 1933 ss 42 and 43
  Permits the use of depositions from child witnesses to certain offences if testifying in court would involve serious danger to the child's health.

Miscellaneous exceptions that exist after the Criminal Justice and Public Order Act 1994

- Criminal Justice Act 1967 s 9
  Allows the use of depositions with the agreement of the parties.
- Criminal Justice Act 1988 s 30
  Allows the use of expert opinion reports which are hearsay provided certain conditions are satisfied (see later).
- Bankers' Books Evidence Act 1879 ss 3 and 4
  Sections 3 and 4 allow the use of a bank's books as evidence of matters stated therein.

Computer evidence

If a computer generates hearsay evidence then the provisions of s 23 or s 24 must be satisfied. In addition the evidence must satisfy the requirements in s 69 PACE 1984.

Section 69 requires evidence to be presented to the court that there are no reasonable grounds to believe that the evidence may be inaccurate because of the working of the computer, and that at all material times the computer was operating properly. A malfunctioning that does not affect the reliability of the evidence will not lead to exclusion.

In *R v Shephard* (1993) the House of Lords considered that the requisite evidence under s 69 could be provided by someone with everyday experience of the operation of the computer. There was no need for expert evidence unless there was a suggestion of a technical fault that would require detailed explanation.

Shephard was a case involving the admissibility of a till receipt. The till operator would tap in the product code number at her till, which was linked to a central computer. The till receipt would then show a product description and price. The till receipt was being tendered to show theft, and was accordingly hearsay, since it depended upon human input and was not producing real evidence. Section 69 was satisfied by calling the store detective to explain the operation of the computer system.

The House of Lords went on to say that s 69 must be satisfied whenever computer evidence is used, overruling the case of *R v Spiby* (1990) where the real evidence generated by automatic logging of phone calls had been held to be outside the scope of s 69.

12 The rule against hearsay: civil cases

Introduction

Since trial is by judge alone, there has always been a more relaxed atti-tude to hearsay evidence in civil cases than in criminal cases, where there is concern over the jury's ability to assess hearsay. In the Civil Evidence Act 1968 wide ranging statutory exceptions to the rule against hearsay statements of fact were formulated, and this was extended to hearsay statements of opinion by the Civil Evidence Act 1972.

The Law Commission Report No 216 proposed dramatic new mea-sures which have been implemented in the Civil Evidence Act 1995, which received the Royal Assent in November 1995, and came into force on 31 January 1997.

The Civil Evidence Act 1995

No exclusion of hearsay – s 1

Section 1(1) CEA 1995 provides:

In civil proceedings evidence shall not be excluded on the ground that it is hearsay.

This is a dramatic restatement, which will mean that the hearsay nature of evidence will not lead to exclusion. Rather it will lead to procedural requirements needing to be followed under s 2 CEA 1995.

Statements are any representation of fact or opinion, however made: s 13 CEA 1995.

Hearsay is defined in s 1(2)(a) as 'a statement made otherwise than by a person while giving oral evidence in the proceedings which is tendered as evidence of the matters stated'.

The Act applies to hearsay of any degree: s 1(2)(b).

The notice procedure – s 2

Unless the parties agree to dispense with the s 2 provisions, a party wishing to tender hearsay evidence will need to comply with the notice procedure in s 2. It will be necessary to inform the other party of the intention to rely on hearsay evidence and, if requested, provide such details of the hearsay evidence as are reasonable to allow the practical difficulties of it being hearsay to be addressed by the other party: s 2(1).

Section 2(2) provides for the making of rules of court which will provide detailed guidance on what proceedings the rules apply to, what kind of hearsay can be excluded from the notice requirements, and the way in which notice must be given and any relevant time limits.

Section 2(4) makes it clear that a failure to comply with s 2(1) or (2) does not render the evidence inadmissible, but will affect the weight to be given to the evidence, and can also lead to costs penalties.

The power to call the witness – s 3

Where a party proposes to adduce a hearsay statement by a witness without the witness being called to give oral evidence, they will run the risk that their opponent will be allowed to call the witness.

Section 3 will allow rules of court to be made which will enable the opponent to call the witness who made the hearsay statement being tendered and cross-examine that witness even though they have given no oral evidence in chief. This will require leave from the trial judge and the hearsay statement of the witness is treated as the witness' examination in chief.

Relevant considerations to determine weight of hearsay evidence – s 4

Section 4 sets out a statutory set of criteria by which the weight of the hearsay evidence may be judged. Section 4(1) allows the court to take into account any circumstances that can reasonably lead to inferences of reliability or unreliability being drawn. It also makes it clear that in some circumstances there may be no weight to the evidence.

Section 4(2) lists specific criteria that can be taken into account:

Regard may be had, in particular, to the following:

(a) Whether it would have been reasonable and practicable for the party by whom the evidence was adduced to have produced the maker of the original statement as a witness;

(b) whether the original statement was made contemporaneously with the occurrence or existence of the matters stated;

(c) whether the evidence involves multiple hearsay;

(d) whether any person involved had any motive to conceal or misrepresent matters;

(e) whether the original statement was an edited account or was made in collaboration with another or for a particular purpose;

(f) whether the circumstances in which the evidence is adduced as hearsay are such as to suggest an attempt to prevent a proper evaluation of its weight.

This seems to suggest a preference for oral evidence if it is readily available, with less weight being given to hearsay statements where the maker could easily have been called to testify. Generally, the closer in time to the event or matter that the statement was made, the better. The more removed hearsay statements will carry less weight, unless there are safeguards in place to prevent each repetition becoming less accurate. Motive will play an important part in assessing weight, as will possible collusion. The danger of inaccuracy from edited accounts must be borne in mind, together with any behaviour that might be viewed as preventing a realistic assessment of weight.

Competence and credibility – s 5

It will not be possible to admit hearsay statements made or communicated by someone who would have been an incompetent witness at the time they made the statement: s 5(1). This means that a statement by an adult who would fail the test of civil competence because of mental or physical infirmity or lack of understanding is inadmissible. Statements by children are admissible if the child satisfies the s 96(1) Children Act 1989 test for unsworn evidence.

Section 5(2) permits the credibility of the maker of the hearsay statement to be attacked, including the use of previous inconsistent statements made by them. It does not allow, however, the use of evidence that would have been inadmissible to rebut the witness' answer in cross-examination. (This is designed to prevent an explosion of collateral issues.)

Previous statements of witnesses – s 6

Section 6(1) states that the provisions of the Act apply to previous statements made by persons who *are* called as witnesses. Such previous statements are only admissible with leave of the court (s 6(2)), unless they are being used to rebut a suggestion of recent fabrication. (This does not extend to preventing a witness statement from being adopted by the witness.) Previous statements, if admissible, can be admitted as evidence of the matters stated: s 6(5).

Section 6(3) preserves the position regarding previous inconsistent statements made by the witness under ss 3, 4, 5 of the Criminal Procedure Act 1865. Such statements can be evidence of matters stated: s 6(5).

Section 6(4) preserves the position regarding memory refreshing documents and when they become evidence. If such a statement does become evidence, it is admissible as evidence of the matters stated: s 6(5).

Evidence admissible at common law – s 7

Section 7(1) provides that the old s 9 CEA 1968 exception in relation to admissions has been superseded by the Act. This means that admissions will be admissible by virtue of s 1 CEA 1995. Normally notice is required for hearsay under s 2, but this will not be required for admissions when the rules of court come into effect, since s 2(2)(a) allows the exempting of certain kinds of statement from the requirement of notice.

The other common law exceptions preserved in s 9 CEA 1968 are preserved in s 7(2) and s 7(3).

Section 7(2) provides that the following shall continue to be admissible as evidence of facts stated in them:

(a) published works dealing with matters of a public nature (for example, histories, scientific works, dictionaries and maps);

(b) public documents (for example public registers and returns made under public authority with respect to matters of public interest);

(c) records (for example the records of certain courts, treaties, Crown grants, pardons and commissions).

Section 7(3) preserves the common law rules allowing the court to treat evidence as proving or disproving matters where:

(a) evidence of a person's reputation is admissible for the purpose of proving his good or bad character; or

(b) evidence of reputation or family tradition is admissible:

(i) for the purpose of proving or disproving pedigree or the existence of a marriage; or

(ii) for the purpose of proving or disproving the existence of any public or general right or of identifying any person or thing.

The notice procedure and ss 2–6 do not apply to hearsay that is admissible through the common law exceptions preserved in s 7(2) and (3), s 2(4).

Proof of statements in documents – s 8

If a statement is contained in a document, it can be proved by using the original document, or an authenticated copy: s 8(1). It does not matter how many stages removed the copy is from the original; the copy can be a copy of a copy: s 8(2).

Proof of records of business or public authority – s 9

Section 9(1) provides that documents that are shown to form part of business or public authority records are admissible without further proof. A document will form part of such a record if the court is shown a signed certificate to that effect by an officer of the business or public authority: s 9(2)

Section 9(3) allows the use of an affidavit by an officer of the business or authority to establish the absence of an entry in his records, the so called negative hearsay situation.

Section 9(4) is a definition section:

- 'records' means records in whatever form;
- 'business' includes any activity regularly carried on over a period of time, whether for profit or not, by anybody (whether corporate or not) or by an individual;
- 'officer' includes any person occupying a responsible position in relation to the relevant activities of the business or public authority or in relation to its records;
- 'public authority includes any public or statutory undertaking, any government department and any person holding office under Her Majesty.

The court has a power, depending on the circumstances of a case to dispense with any of the s 9 requirements for a particular document: s 9(5).

Proof of actuarial tables in personal injury and FAA claims – s 10

Section 10 renders Ogden tables admissible in order to calculate future financial loss on an actuarial basis.

Meaning of civil proceedings – ss 11 and 12

Civil proceedings means proceedings in any court or tribunal where strict rules of evidence apply: s 11. It is also possible for the Act to apply to arbitration: s 12.

Interpretation – s 13

'Document' means anything in which information of any description is recorded.

Various other phrases are also defined, but have been dealt with already.

Note: the provisions in the CEA 1968 s 5 in relation to computer evidence have been repealed and there is nothing in the new CEA 1995 to replace them. Therefore computer hearsay is treated in the same way as other forms of hearsay.

13 Confessions

ESSENTIALS

You should be familiar with the following areas:	✓
• definition of a confession	
• exclusion under s 76	
• exclusion under s 78	
• exclusion under s 82	
• the effect of exclusion	
• excluding other improperly obtained evidence under s 78	

Introduction

A confession is defined in s 82(1) PACE 1984 as 'including any statement wholly or partly adverse to the person who made it, whether made to a person in authority or not and whether made in words or otherwise'.

At common law such a statement is admissible against the maker as an exception to the rule against hearsay, since it is thought that adverse remarks are more likely to be true than self-serving exculpatory remarks. This common law principle is preserved in s 76(1) PACE 1984.

However, research and bitter experience of miscarriages of justice suggest that incriminatory remarks may not always be true, and that safeguards are needed to prevent confessions being obtained and used improperly. These statutory safeguards are found in the Police and Criminal Evidence Act 1984 and the detailed codes of practice made from time to time under the power in s 66 PACE.

The nature of a confession

There is no need for the statement to be completely incriminatory in order to amount to a confession, provided that it does have some incriminatory material. The incriminatory nature of the confession must be judged at the time the statement was made (*R v Sat Bhambra* (1988)), and statements that were exculpatory at the time they were made cannot be viewed as confessions because of subsequent developments, such as their being inconsistent with the defence run at the trial.

The definition covers remarks made to persons in authority or otherwise, and would include incriminatory statements made to friends or family, as well as those to the police or others investigating offences. However, it is important that the statement can be regarded as incriminatory; if it is ambiguous, so that it cannot safely be regarded as an admission, it should be excluded. In *R v Schofield* (1917) the statement 'just my luck' on being approached by the police could not be a reliable indication of guilt.

Statements made in words or otherwise are capable of amounting to a confession, and this could cover oral and written statements as well as gestures and conduct. In *Li Shu Ling v The Queen* (1989) this was used to admit a filmed reconstruction of the crime that the accused had willingly taken part in to demonstrate how he had committed the crime, but which was contrary to his defence at trial.

Excluding confessions

It is possible to challenge the admissibility of confessions under s 76 PACE 1984 and following the case of *R v Mason* (1988) confessions can also be excluded under the provisions of s 78. The usual procedure for challenging confessions is that defence counsel indicates to prosecution counsel before the trial begins that the admissibility of the confession, or indeed any other disputed evidence, will be challenged. Prosecuting counsel will then not mention the disputed evidence in the presence of the jury until admissibility has been determined.

Admissibility is usually determined by the judge in the absence of the jury. Legal argument will be presented and sometimes witnesses may be called in which case the procedure is known as a *voir dire*, or trial within a trial. In some cases this will take place at the beginning of the trial, in others issues of admissibility will be determined when they arise in the course of the trial.

In the case of confessions, the defence may dispute that the confession was ever made. This is essentially a factual dispute, and is determined by the jury and not by the judge on a *voir dire*: *Ajodha v The State* (1982). However, where the defence make allegations of impropriety in relation to a confession then, according to *Ajodha*, it is for the defence to choose whether to argue this in the absence of the jury on the *voir dire*, or in the presence of the jury. The *voir dire* has the advantage that the jury never hear the disputed evidence unless it is ruled admissible, but occasionally this can give prosecution witnesses the opportunity to 'rehearse' their evidence, and look more credible on the point when their evidence is presented to the jury.

However, the comments in *Ajodha* have to be considered in the light of s 76(2) of PACE 1984 which seems to indicate that challenges to the admissibility of a confession on the basis that it was obtained by oppression or in circumstances that are likely to make it unreliable must be made on a *voir dire*: *R v Oxford Justices Ex Parte Berry* (1988).

If the defendant testifies on the *voir dire* and this results in the confession being excluded then no mention can be made during the main trial of his remarks on the *voir dire*, even if they are inconsistent with his defence at the trial: *Wong Kam Ming v R* (1980) and *R v Brophy* (1982).

Challenging admissibility under s 76

Section 76(2) applies to confessions that the prosecution propose to rely on, and provides that where the defence represent 'that the confession was or may have been obtained:

(a)   by oppression of the person who made it; or

(b)   in consequence of anything said or done which was likely, in the circumstances existing at the time, to render unreliable any confession which might be made by him in consequence thereof.

the court shall not allow the confession to be given in evidence against him except in so far as the prosecution proves to the court beyond reasonable doubt that the confession (notwithstanding that it may be true) was not obtained as aforesaid'.

Therefore once the defence make the representation the prosecution have the legal burden of disproving oppression or unreliability beyond reasonable doubt, and even confessions that are true can be excluded. There is a further provision in s 76(3) for the judge to put the prosecution to proof even though the defence made no representation about the confession.

Oppression

Oppression is defined in s 76(8) to include 'torture, inhuman or degrading treatment, the use or threat of violence'. This has been further developed by case law, and in essence requires impropriety on the part of the person in authority. In *R v Fulling* (1987) the defendant was upset when the police told her that her boyfriend was having an affair. The court cited the dictionary definition with approval requiring evidence of 'exercise of power in a burdensome, harsh or wrongful manner; unjust or cruel treatment of subjects ... the imposition of unreasonable or unjust burdens'. This was not present, there was no 'impropriety ... oppression actively applied in an improper manner by the police'.

R v Fulling sets a high standard for behaviour to amount to oppression, a mere breach of the codes of practice is unlikely to be oppressive. In *R v Miller, Paris and Others* (1993) the defendant, Miller, along with others, was suspected of being involved in the murder of a prostitute. The defendant was of low IQ and was interviewed for over 13 hours. The tenor of the interview was very aggressive, with persistent repetition of the same allegation over 300 times, which the defendant had denied. There was a denial of access to legal advice, and after constant badgering the defendant confessed. The persistent bullying nature of the questioning was held to be oppressive.

This does not mean that the police cannot interview at length, or repeat allegations, or raise their voices. In *R v Emmerson* (1990) a police officer lost his temper, shouted and swore at the suspect in a manner that was held not to be oppressive.

Unreliability

In order to exclude a confession on this basis there must be something said or done by persons other than the defendant. In *R v Goldenberg* (1989) the defendant argued his confession was unreliable because he was a drug addict, a fact unknown to the police, and had confessed in order to be able to get more drugs. This was not capable of being a basis for exclusion since the confession was unreliable because of the defendant's inherent drug dependency and not through anything done or said by the police. However, if there is something said or done, then the defendant's inherent characteristics can be the explanation for why the confession may be unreliable, as in *R v Everett*, where the defendant's mental condition made his confession in the face of police questioning likely to be unreliable.

The things said or done do not have to amount to impropriet: *R v Fulling* (1987). However, clearly, breaches of the Codes of Practice can be evidence of things done: *R v Delaney* (1988).

It is then necessary to consider whether a confession in those circumstances is likely to be unreliable. It is irrelevant that the actual confession is true and reliable. The facts of *R v Fulling* would not demonstrate unreliability since a woman is not likely to confess to a crime she did not commit on being told of her boyfriend's affair. Her accusations against him or his new girlfriend might be unreliable, but the implication of herself would not be!

A case where unreliability did exist was *R v Harvey* (1988). The defendant was slightly mentally retarded and was being questioned with her lesbian lover about the murder of a man. The lover admitted responsibility, at which point the defendant confessed that the crime was entirely the defendant's responsibility. It was likely that a confession in such circumstances was unreliable, as the defendant might well lie to protect her lover.

The causal link

It must be shown that the oppression or thing said or done caused the confession to be made. In *R v Smith* (1959) there was a causal link between the oppressive treatment of the suspect by his commanding officer and his first confession, which was excluded. However, once the suspect had been removed from that custody, and was being questioned by investigating officers his second confession was unaffected by the first oppression and so could be admitted.

Exclusion of confessions under s 78

The general discretion to exclude prosecution evidence under s 78 if it would have an adverse effect on the fairness of proceedings can also be used to exclude confessions. In *R v Mason* (1988) the police tricked the defendant by telling him, in the presence of his solicitor, that they had evidence of his fingerprints on a bottle that linked him with an arson attack. The defendant confessed, and although his confession could not be excluded under s 76 since there was no oppression or unreliability, it could be excluded under s 78. Such blatant lies and trickery by the police could not be condoned by the court, especially since this was really the only evidence against the defendant.

Even an innocent misleading of the defendant about the evidence the police have against him has led to exclusion under s 78: *R v Kwabena Poku* (1978).

It is important to have an understanding of the main provisions of the Codes of Practice, especially Code C, as they relate to the detention and interrogation of suspects. These provisions contain important safeguards for the suspect, and should ensure that he is treated humanely, with proper rest, food, clothing and heat. Interviews should be properly recorded on tape or video, and significant silences or statements made outside interviews should be mentioned at the first opportunity at a subsequent taped interview. Suspects should be cautioned before interview and allowed access to legal advice. They should also be allowed to inform someone of their arrest and not subjected to improper searches or taking of samples. There are time limits on detention before charge, and provisions for proper reviews of detention.

Whilst a breach of the codes does not automatically lead to exclusion, since the function of s 78 is not to discipline the police, *R v Delaney* (1988), it is important to check whether any provisions have been breached. The more serious or numerous the breaches are, the more likely the evidence will be excluded: *R v Keenan* (1989). If the police act in deliberate bad faith, this will also tend to exclude the evidence: *R v Walsh* (1990).

Access to legal advice

Section 58 gives a suspect the right to consult privately with a solicitor, which may be one of his own choosing, or the duty solicitor. He must be informed of this right, both orally and by way of written notice, and told that the duty solicitor is independent of the police and available free of charge. If a suspect requests a solicitor he must be allowed to consult as soon as practicable unless access can be delayed by virtue of s 58. Delay is only possible for serious arrestable offences on the authorisation of a superintendent or above. There must be reasonable grounds for believing that access would interfere with or harm evidence or persons, or alert other suspects, or hinder recovery of property. It is not a good reason for delaying access to say that solicitors make obtaining confessions more difficult for the police!

In *R v Samuel* (1988) severe limitation was placed on the use of s 58 in that it was held that since solicitors are professional people it is extremely unlikely that access to a solicitor would lead to any of the reasons for delay being satisfied. Only if the suspect asked for a solicitor who was known to be a risk, or who employed persons in his office who might deliberately or inadvertently bring about one of the situations in s 58 would delay be acceptable. Even then the suspect should be allowed access to an alternative solicitor. Delay cannot exceed 36 hours.

In *R v Samuel* the evidence was excluded since there was a breach of s 58, but in *R v Alladice* (1988), although there was a breach there was no exclusion of evidence because the suspect was an experienced criminal who knew his rights and had not been disadvantaged by the delay in access.

Covert police operations

In some cases the police resort to using undercover police officers to obtain evidence, and may secretly bug the defendant's remarks. In *R v Khan* (1996) the House of Lords acknowledged that there is no rule preventing the admissibility of covert recordings as such, even if this involved the police in bugging a suspect's house as in *R v Khan*, or a police cell, as in *R v Bailey* (1993). However, both these cases involved the secret recording of a suspect's remarks, but without the police being involved in questioning the suspect. This was just a form of electronic eavesdropping, and in life there is no guarantee that one's remarks will not be overheard.

Cases where the police have secretly recorded the defendant's responses to questions have been treated differently. An interview is where questions are asked of someone the police suspect of an offence with a view to obtaining incriminatory responses (*R v Christou* (1992)), and such interviews should be conducted with the protection of the codes of practice, ie proper contemporaneous records, presence of solicitor, cautioning of the suspect, etc. Therefore questioning a suspect without telling him that his answers are being recorded and may be used against him can lead to exclusion.

In *R v Stagg* (1995) the suspect was suspected by the police of being involved in a murder of a young woman. A woman police officer started a friendship with the suspect to see if the police could obtain any evidence to use against him. She and the suspect exchanged increasingly intimate letters, where the suspect finally stated an interest in the kind of perverted sadistic activity that might link him to the murder. The use of the police officer to form a friendship with the view to obtaining incriminatory material was condemned by the trial judge and the evidence was excluded. Likewise in *R v Hall* (1995) a police officer formed a romantic attachment with a murder suspect and his confession during a conversation to her that he had killed his wife was ruled inadmissible. The police were improperly questioning with a view to obtaining incriminatory evidence and the use of romantic relationships was to be discouraged.

Contrast these cases with *R v Smurthwaite* (1994) where the defendant had been seeking someone to act as a contract killer. A police officer posed as such a person, and was told by the defendant what to do. This was secretly recorded and the tape held to be admissible. The police officer was not encouraging the defendant to commit a crime he would otherwise not commit, and the police officer's role was purely passive. There had been no improper interviewing, the suspect had volunteered the information, and since there was a good record of what had been said it was admissible.

Other exclusionary discretion

The common law rule in *R v Sang* (1980) is preserved in s 82(3) and therefore it is possible to excluded evidence of a confession if its prejudicial effect outweighs its probative value.

The consequences of exclusion for the prosecution

If a confession is excluded, it cannot be used by the prosecution to prove the truth of its contents. However, the confession may have led the prosecution to find other evidence. This other evidence, the so called 'fruits of the poisoned tree' is admissible, s 76(4) although the prosecution cannot say that it was discovered as a result of what the defendant said, unless the defence have already mentioned this, s 76(5). A confession can also be used for the purpose of showing that the defendant speaks, writes or expresses himself in a particular way.

This means that if a confession has been excluded because of oppression, but in the confession the defendant tells the police where they will find the murder weapon, then the finding of the murder weapon will be admissible. However, the police cannot say they found the weapon where the defendant said they would. The value of this evidence will vary, depending on where the weapon was found. If it was found hidden under the defendant's mattress this will tend to be weighty circumstantial evidence of his involvement; if found in a litter bin at Oxford Circus it will not implicate the defendant at all. Likewise the confession could be used to show the defendant misspells certain words if this is relevant, or that he uses certain unusual but relevant expressions.

The consequence of exclusion for a co-accused

Although a confession may be excluded as part of the prosecution case, this does not prevent its use by a co-accused if the defendant's confession has a relevance to the co-accused's defence: *R v Rowson* (1989).

In *R v Myers* (1996) the Court of Appeal upheld the view that even though a confession may be inadmissible for the prosecution because of breaches of the codes of practice, it may still be admissible for the co-accused. In this case the defendant and co-accused were accused of a murder that could only have been committed by one or both of them. Noone else could have committed the crime. The defendant confessed to the police that she was responsible, and the confession was a voluntary confession, albeit in breach of the codes of practice. These breaches did not stop the use of the defendant's confession by the co-accused since it was supportive of the co-accused's case that the defendant was solely responsible.

Editing of confessions

A confession is admissible against the maker, and not anyone else implicated in the confession. However, it is often the case that a defendant's confession contains remarks that damage his co-accused. It might be possible to edit out such references: *R v Silcott, Braithwaite and*

Others (1987). However, it is not possible to delete references to a co-accused at the expense of the defendant's defence. In such cases the judge should direct the jury that what the defendant said in his confession is evidence against him only, and not evidence against a co-accused.

Confessions can also be edited to delete reference to ii ...... ible evidence, such as where a defendant makes remarks about his bad character or being known to the police: *R v Knight* (1946).

Exclusion of other improperly obtained evidence under s 78

Section 78 applies to any sort of evidence tendered by the prosecution, and it may be that breaches of the law in PACE and the Codes of Practice will lead to the exclusion of such evidence. It is necessary to convince the judge to exercise his discretion to exclude on the basis that the evidence would have an adverse effect on the fairness of proceedings if admitted. Again, the seriousness of the breach, the good or bad intentions of the police are relevant considerations. So, for example, evidence discovered during an improper search of premises may be excluded in some cases.

Particular problems arise in the use of undercover police operations, or the agent provocateur. In *R v Christou and Wright* (1992) the police set up a jewellery shop and the defendants were caught trying to sell stolen jewellery in the bogus shop. The evidence was admissible. The police had not encouraged the defendants to commit a crime they otherwise would not. The deception occurred after the offence had been committed, with the police playing a passive role, with no improper questioning. Likewise in *R v Williams* (1993) the police used a lorry loaded with cigarette cartons, and recorded the actions of the defendants who tried to steal them. This recording of the commission of the crime was admissible. There had been no pressure on the defendants to act as they did, and there was therefore no adverse effect on the fairness of proceedings.

14 Silence of the defendant

ESSENTIALS

You should be familiar with the following areas:

- failure to testify: s 35
- failure to mention facts relied on in defence: s 34
- failure to account for incriminating objects, substances and marks: s 36
- failure to account for presence in an incriminator's place
- failure to provide samples

Common law

At common law the defendant's silence in the face of accusations could in certain circumstances amount to an acceptance of those allegations (see Chapter 10). This was easier to show in the case of accusations made by an ordinary person than in the case of accusations made by the police, where acceptance by silence was very rare.

Statute

The provisions of the Criminal Justice and Public Order Act 1994 make dramatic alterations to the effect of the defendant's silence both before and during the trial. The provisions of s 35 that relate to the defendant's failure to testify or answer questions at trial have been dealt with in Chapter 2. The remaining provisions that alter the effect of silence are to be found in ss 34, 36 and 37 of the Act.

Section 34 CJPOA 1994 – failure to mention facts relied on in defence

At common law there was no requirement for the defence to give advance notice to the prosecution of the type of defence that was to be run at trial, save for the need to give an alibi notice. The defendant who failed to mention the line of his defence could not have adverse inferences drawn against him: *R v Gilbert* (1977). This was subject to judicial criticism and the Criminal Law Revision Committee recommended altering the rule in their 1972 report. However, nothing was done and the Royal Commission on Criminal Justice in 1993 thought that there should be no obligation on the defence to raise issues relevant to their defence at any time before the prosecution had given advance disclosure of the prosecution case. The Royal Commission thought it would be wrong to draw adverse inferences from a defendant's failure to mention facts to the police that he later mentions in his defence.

Contents of s 34

Section 34 ignores the advice of the Royal Commission and provides for the drawing of adverse inferences from a failure to mention facts later relied on by the defence. Section 34(1) provides:

> Where, in any proceedings against a person for an offence, evidence is given that the accused:
>
> (a) at any time before he was charged with the offence, on being questioned under caution by a constable trying to discover whether or by whom the offence had been committed, failed to mention any fact relied on in his defence in those proceedings; or
>
> (b) on being charged with the offence or officially informed that he might be prosecuted for it, failed to mention any such fact,
>
> being a fact which in the circumstances existing at the time the accused could reasonably have been expected to mention when being so questioned, charged or informed, as the case may be, subsection (2) applies.

Section 34(2) allows the court to 'draw such inferences as appear proper'.

Section 34(4) extends the provisions to questioning by persons other than the police if they are charged with the duty of investigating offences or charging offenders.

Need for caution

Section 34 applies to questioning on caution before charge or on the defendant being charged or informed officially of the prospect of being prosecuted. Thus a failure to mention facts before a suspect is cautioned cannot lead to the drawing of adverse inferences. The new caution is found in Code C para 10.4, which provides for the suspect to be told:

You do not have to say anything. But it may harm your defence if you do not mention when questioned something that you later rely on in court. Anything you do say may be given in evidence.

Usually such questioning will take place in the police station, and be tape-recorded as an interview under Code E. However, if the questioning occurs outside a formal taped interview, what is sometimes termed a 'verbal', then the new codes of practice require the police to mention at the beginning of a subsequent taped interview that they asked questions of the accused and what his response, or lack of response was. This applies in the case of a 'significant statement or silence' which is defined as one which appears capable of being used in evidence against the suspect: Code C para 11.2A. The accused is then asked to confirm or deny this and whether he wishes to add anything.

Facts that should be mentioned
Inferences can only be drawn if the defendant failed to mention a fact that he later relies on at trial. If he does nothing at trial that goes beyond a denial of the prosecution case, then no adverse inferences can be drawn.

It is also necessary to show that the fact not mentioned is one that the defendant could have reasonably mentioned. What this means is not yet clear, but it presumably would require the accused to have enough knowledge of the police case to know what accusations he has to answer, and can also be affected by the characteristics of the accused himself, such as his age, mental handicap or intoxication that may affect his ability to mention facts.

Inferences that can be drawn
The effect of failing to mention such facts is not clear. The Act talks of the drawing of such inferences as may seem proper, and this could arguably include an inference of guilt. It has been argued that at best s 34 allows the drawing of an inference that the defence raised at trial is an invention of a recent nature, and cannot be believed, rather than a clear cut inference of guilt. In *R v Connolly* (1994) and *R v Campbell* (1993) the Court of Appeal interpreted a similar provision in Northern Ireland legislation and held that the failure of the accused to mention facts later relied on meant that his account of events was a 'recent and false invention'.

There can be no conviction based on the accused's silence alone: s 38 CJPOA 1994.

In *R v Argent* (1996) the Court of Appeal laid down six steps that had to be satisfied before the jury could draw adverse inferences from a defendant's failure to mention facts later relied on in his defence:

- Section 34 only applies if there are proceedings against the defendant for an offence.
- The failure to mention facts must have occurred before the defendant was charged with an offence and not after.
- The failure must arise in questioning under caution by a police constable or other person charged with investigating offences.
- The questioning had to be with a view to finding out whether an alleged offence had been committed, or who was responsible.
- The defendant had to raise a fact in his defence, which he had failed to mention in questioning.
- It is then necessary to consider whether this fact is one that the defendant could reasonably be expected to mention. The time at which this is to be judged is at the time of the questioning and all the circumstances of the case should not be too restrictively construed. The test is a subjective one, based on that particular defendant, not on the hypothetical, reasonable defendant. The time of day, the defendant's age, experience, mental abilities, tiredness, sobriety, personality and the legal advice received were examples of the factors that could be taken into account. This was not an exhaustive list.

The jury need to consider these circumstances and use their common-sense as to whether, on the facts, there was a failure to mention facts relied on in the defence, such that adverse inferences could be drawn.

In *R v Condron* (1996) the defendant and his wife refused to answer questions at the police station on the advice of their solicitor. They were both drug addicts and the solicitor considered that their ability to answer questions might have been affected by their drug-taking. The medical evidence did not suggest that this was in fact the case. At trial they raised facts in their defence that could have been mentioned at the interview. The court considered that the judge was correct in telling the jury that it was for them to decide whether or not to draw adverse inferences, and the fact that the defendants were following legal advice did not prevent the drawing of inferences. It would all turn on the reason for the advice, and it would be unlikely that a mere assertion that the defendant was acting on legal advice would operate to prevent the drawing of adverse inferences. It might, therefore, be necessary for the accused to waive his legal professional privilege and have himself and his solicitor testify as to the reason for the advice to remain silent.

Section 36 – failure to account for incriminating objects, substances and marks

Contents of s 36

Section 36(1) provides:

Where:

(a) a person is arrested by a constable, and there is:

    (i) on his person; or

    (ii) in or on his clothing or footwear; or

    (iii) otherwise in his possession; or

    (iv) in any place in which he is at the time of his arrest,

    any object, substance or mark, or there is a mark on any such object; and

(b) that, or another, constable investigating the case reasonably believes that the presence of the object, substance or mark may be attributable to the participation of the person arrested in the commission of the offence specified by the constable; and

(c) the constable informs the person arrested that he so believes, and requests him to account for the presence of the object, substance or mark; and

(d) the person fails or refuses to do so,

then, if in any proceedings against the person for the offence so specified, evidence of those matters is given ...

Section 36(2) provides that 'the court or jury ... may draw such inferences from the failure or refusal as appear proper'.

Effect of s 36

Section 36 only applies once a suspect has been arrested and informed that the constable believes the substance etc points to the accused's involvement in an offence. The suspect must be told this in everyday language, asked to give an explanation, and told of the consequences of failing to explain. Code C paras 10.5A and 10.5B deal with the special warnings required, and a record should be made of the interview which may be given in evidence at trial.

Section 36 only applies to substances, etc that are present at the time of arrest, not at any other time.

Proper inferences can be drawn from a failure to explain. This will vary from case to case; in some cases a strong adverse inference may be justified, whereas in others there will be less justification for drawing adverse inferences. Much will depend on the incriminatory nature of the substance or mark that the accused is asked to explain.

It is not possible to infer guilt solely through the accused's failure to provide an explanation: s 38(3).

Section 37 – failure to account for presence in an incriminatory place

Contents of s 37

Section 37(1) provides:

Where:

(a) A person arrested by a constable was found by him at a place at or about the time the offence for which he was arrested is alleged to have been committed; and

(b) that or another constable investigating the offence reasonably believes that the presence of the person at that place and at that time may be attributable to his participation in the commission of the offence,

the constable must then inform the suspect of his belief (as with s 36), and then a failure or refusal to account for the presence can be given in evidence, and proper inferences can be drawn from a refusal.

Effect of s 37

Section 37 only applies where the accused is arrested at or near the scene of the alleged crime, and it is only his presence there that explanation can be called for. He does not have to explain his presence elsewhere or at other times, even if this would be relevant to the prosecution case. As with s 36 an explanation in ordinary language of the constable's belief, what account is required and the consequences of failing to explain must be given.

The nature of the inferences that can be drawn will vary from case to case, and silence cannot be the sole basis of finding the defendant guilty: s 38(3).

The defendant's lies

The defendant who has told lies will find that this counts against him in two possible ways. It can affect his credibility, and make the jury less likely to believe his version of events, or it can go further and be indicative of guilt. In certain circumstances, therefore the lie may be circumstantial evidence of the defendant's guilt.

For a lie to indicate guilt it must satisfy the criteria in *R v Lucas* (1981):

- It must be a *deliberate* lie, relate to a material issue and the motive for the lie must be realisation of guilt and fear of the truth.
- The *motive* for lying is very important. There may be a number of reasons why a defendant has lied; he may be scared, wishing to protect someone, or ashamed of his behaviour. Only lies told to conceal his guilt by misleading the police can be indicative of guilt, and it would be wrong to suggest that every lie indicates guilt.

R v Lucas was a corroboration case, and for a lie to corroborate it must be shown to be a lie from a source other than the witness needing corroboration. However, the *Lucas* direction is applicable to cases where corroboration is not needed, and in *R v Goodway* (1993) the court called for a *Lucas* direction to be given whenever the prosecution wish to use a lie by the defendant either in or out of court as supporting the defendant's guilt.

A *Lucas* direction is not needed if the lie is being used to damage the defendant's credibility only: *R v Smith* (1995).

In *R v Burge* (1995) it was suggested that the judge should give a *Lucas* direction if the defence were running an alibi defence, if there was a need for the jury to look for supporting or corroborating evidence which might take the form of lies, or where the prosecution was relying on a lie to prove guilt. It would also be good practice if there was a risk that the jury might take a lie to indicate guilt to consult with counsel to see if a *Lucas* direction was called for.

A lie can only indicate guilt if the defendant admits having lied, or if the prosecution can prove that he lied beyond reasonable doubt, and the motive for lying is to conceal his guilt.

Refusal to provide samples

If the police request a suspect to provide a non-intimate sample within s 63 PACE 1984, and the suspect refuses, then in certain cases the police can take the sample without the suspect's consent (see Chapter 8). There is nothing in the statute that specifies whether a refusal to provide the sample can be used against the defendant, unlike s 62. Under the old law there was no power to take a sample without the suspect's consent, and so a refusal to supply a sample could incriminate the defendant in appropriate cases: *R v Smith* (1985). It is unclear whether this is still the case, but it would seem unlikely given that s 62 provides for adverse inferences to be drawn in relation to intimate samples, but s 63 is silent in relation to non-intimate samples.

Intimate samples are governed by s 62 PACE and cannot be taken without the suspect's consent. However, s 62(10) specifically provides that a refusal to supply an intimate sample without good cause can lead to inferences being drawn. The suspect is warned about this specifically, and therefore a refusal can be taken into account at trial.

15 Opinion evidence

Witnesses should usually testify as to facts that they have perceived, and it is the role of the court to form opinions and to speculate on these facts. Objection can be taken to a line of questioning that appears to be asking the witness to express an opinion, although opinion evidence is admissible if it qualifies as expert opinion evidence, eye witness opinion, or opinion of general reputation.

Expert opinion evidence

Courts deal with an enormous variety of cases, many of them involving highly specialised issues, on which the court needs assistance from properly qualified expert witnesses.

Proper qualification

Only those witnesses who are properly qualified can give evidence as experts. The party calling the witness will normally briefly run through the basis of the witness' qualification as an expert before asking the witness to comment on the facts. Qualification can come from formal qualification but it does not need to. There are some areas where qualification can come from experience and skill acquired over a number of years, as in *R v Silverlock* (1894) where a solicitor who had studied handwriting as a hobby for many years gave expert opinion evidence concerning some handwriting. However in very technical areas where formal qualifications are available, it will be unlikely that someone lacking such qualifications would be regarded as an expert: *R v Inch* (1989) where the evidence of a medical orderly was inadmissible. However, in *R v Oakley* (1979), the evidence of a police officer with many years experience of road traffic accidents was admissible opinion evidence on the possible causes of the accident.

Subject-matter of opinion beyond the competence of the court

Expert opinion evidence should only be admitted if it concerns matters beyond the normal competence of the court. Matters that are within the court's experience should be left to the court to form an opinion.

In *R v Anderson* (1972) the defendant was accused of obscenity offences. The test for obscenity is whether the material would tend to corrupt or deprave, and this is not a proper matter for expert opinion. The effect of the material on adults is within the experience of the courts, although in *DPP v A and BC Chewing Gum* (1968) the obscene nature of chewing gum cards and their effects on children were proper matters for expert opinion evidence.

The reliability of ordinary witnesses and the likelihood of them telling the truth is a matter for the court. However, expert evidence will be admissible as to the reliability of statements by persons of abnormal susceptibility (*R v Silcott, Braithwaite and Raghip* (1991)), or the reliability of a person suffering from medical conditions affecting their ability to tell the truth (*Toohey v MPC* (1965)).

Highly technical matters will clearly be proper areas for expert evidence, as in *Folkes v Chadd* (1782) where evidence was given as to the possible causes of silting in a harbour. Other common uses of expert evidence are for forensic matters and the nature and extent of a plaintiff's disabilities and prognosis for recovery in personal injury cases.

In criminal cases expert evidence will not be admissible to show the likely reaction, intention or behaviour of a defendant who can be regarded as a normal man. Whereas such evidence will be admissible if the defendant is being portrayed as a man with abnormal qualities or propensities. Consequently, provocation (*R v Turner* (1975)), intention (*R v Chard* (1971)), credibility (*R v Mackenney* (1981)), and drunkenness (*R v Tandy* (1989)) are all matters for the court to decide. However, insanity (*R v Holmes* (1871)), diminished responsibility (*R v Bailey* (1977)), automatism (*Bratty v AG* (1963)) are all matters for expert opinion.

The ultimate issue

At common law experts were required to avoid expressing an opinion on the ultimate issue, ie the issue the court had to determine. However, in civil cases the rule is abolished by s 3 Civil Evidence Act 1972, which provides that the expert can express an opinion on any matter he is qualified to speak on. In criminal cases the rule has not been abolished but in *DPP v A and BC Chewing Gum* (1968) the court held that the judge could allow the expert to express an opinion on the ultimate issue, as long as there was no risk of prejudice to the defendant through the jury giving undue weight to the expert's opinion on the ultimate issue. The jury must be told that the actual determination of the ultimate issue is for them not the expert.

The basis of expert opinion evidence

The expert will often give evidence based on facts perceived by him. It is nonetheless possible for an expert to give opinion evidence where he himself has no knowledge of the facts, but is basing his opinion on facts related to him by others or by documents. In *English Exporters v Eldonwall* (1973) this was stated to be acceptable, provided that the expert evidence was not used to prove the truth of the facts on which it was based. Therefore an expert could look at medical notes of an operation that he was not present at and state that, in his opinion, based on the notes, the operation was carried out improperly. It will then be necessary to prove that the operation did in fact take place in the way alleged either by calling eye witnesses or admitting documentary hearsay.

On many occasions an expert will reach a particular view by reference to articles and research carried out by himself or others. Such material is hearsay technically, but is admissible to explain why the expert formed his view, and to give weight to the expert's evidence: *R v Abadom* (1983); *H v Schering Chemicals* (1983).

Advance notice

In civil cases where it is proposed to rely on expert opinion evidence, RSC Ord 38 rr 36–42 provide for the notice procedure to be followed for expert evidence in the High Court. In the county court CCR Ord 20 r 27 applies.

At trial expert evidence can only be used with leave of the court, or the opponent, unless the party has applied for and complied with directions for disclosure. In many cases automatic directions provide for simultaneous disclosure of expert evidence by both parties.

In criminal cases both prosecution and defence must give advance notice of expert evidence they intend to rely on, including the name of the expert, the contents of their evidence, any research it was based on and any tests carried out.

Hearsay and expert opinion evidence

It is usual for experts to give oral evidence at trial if the matters are contentious, since evidence tested by cross-examination always carries greater weight. However, in civil cases s 1 Civil Evidence Act 1995 renders hearsay statements of fact and opinion admissible, and so an expert report could be used in civil cases, either on its own or in conjunction with the oral evidence of the expert.

In criminal cases s 30 Criminal Justice Act 1988 renders expert reports admissible whether or not the expert gives oral evidence. If the expert does not testify then leave will be needed from the court before the report can be used. In granting leave, the court considers why the expert is not testifying, the risk of unfairness and all the circumstances of the case. Generally uncontroversial evidence may be admitted in report form, and the report is admitted to prove the truth of its contents.

Non-expert opinion evidence: the eye witness account

Many witnesses perceive facts and then go on to communicate those facts by expressing an opinion in a way that is a common sense shorthand observation of facts. Identification evidence, age, drunkenness, and speed are all matters that ordinary witnesses comment on. This is not really opinion evidence as it is a way of describing facts perceived by them.

Such evidence is admissible in civil trials by virtue of s 3(2) Civil Evidence Act 1972, and would also be admissible in criminal trials by reference to the common law.

There is no need to give notice of non-expert eye witness accounts if they are going to be presented orally in court. However, accounts that are being tendered in documents will have to be given the usual notice required for hearsay evidence.

Evidence of general reputation

A person's general reputation can be the subject of opinion evidence from someone who knows him.

16 Use of previous judgments

As a general rule it is not possible for a party in proceedings to seek to admit a previous judgment of another court on another occasion to prove that the facts on which the judgment were based are true. Such a use would technically be hearsay and it could be prejudicial to inform a court what view a previous court took.

However, whilst at common law such judgments are inadmissible (*Hollington v Hewthorn* (1943)), there are certain statutes that make provision for the use of previous judgments. If a party can rely on one of these statutory provisions, then the previous judgment will be admissible.

Civil cases

The appropriate provisions may be found in ss 11, 12 and 13 Civil Evidence Act 1968.

Section 11 – the use of criminal convictions in civil proceedings

Section 11(1) permits the use of previous convictions of a UK court or court martial in a subsequent civil case, provided that the conviction is subsisting and relevant to an issue in the civil proceedings. If an appeal against conviction is pending then it is the usual practice to stay the civil proceedings until the result of the appeal is known.

The conviction cannot be one of a foreign court, but there is no need for the conviction to be that of the parties to the case. Provided the conviction is relevant, it does not matter whose conviction it is. It is quite common for road accidents to lead to a criminal prosecution in which the driver is convicted of dangerous driving. This has proved beyond reasonable doubt that he drove dangerously, which is clearly relevant to the issue of whether he drove negligently when he is subsequently sued for compensation by those injured in the accident. His conviction would also be relevant if the driver was not being sued, but his employers were on the basis of vicarious liability for his tort.

The operation of s 11 saves a party from having to reargue a point, thus saving time and money. There is also little injustice since the behaviour has already been proven beyond reasonable doubt, which more than suffices where proof is only needed on the balance of probabilities.

Section 11(2) provides that the conviction is proof that the person committed the offence for which he or she has been convicted. However s 11(2) is a statutory persuasive presumption, and it is possible that the opponent can rebut the presumption by proving that the conviction was wrong (*Wauchope v Mordecai* (1970)), although this is difficult.

Section 11 does not permit the use of civil judgments in criminal cases, only the use of criminal convictions in civil cases. A party intending to rely on s 11 should plead it.

Section 12 – the use of adultery and paternity findings

Section 12 allows the use of findings of adultery and paternity from previous proceedings to be admissible in the present civil proceedings provided it is relevant to an issue in the proceedings. Again s 12(2) creates a statutory persuasive presumption that the finding is correct unless the contrary is shown. The party seeking to rebut the presumption has the legal burden of proving the earlier finding was wrong. The party relying on s 12 must plead it.

Section 13 – the use of criminal convictions in defamation cases

In defamation proceedings a party can rely on a relevant previous conviction, which is taken as absolute proof that the person committed the offence for which he or she has been convicted. This rule cannot be rebutted and does not need to be pleaded.

Use of previous judgments in criminal cases

Since the standard in civil cases is balance of probabilities, whereas that in a criminal case is beyond reasonable doubt, it is obvious that civil findings cannot be admissible in subsequent criminal proceedings. However, s 74 PACE 1984 does contain provisions permitting the use of previous criminal convictions in later criminal cases.

The convictions of others

Section 74(1) provides for the admissibility of a valid and subsisting conviction of a person other than the defendant. This conviction must be one of a UK court or court martial and includes a guilty plea by a co-accused: *R v Golder* (1960).

The conviction of the other person must be relevant to an issue in the present criminal proceedings. The question of whether the conviction is relevant has proved to be a problematic one, and there is a real risk that the defendant could be unfairly prejudiced by the admissibility of the convictions of others.

In *R v O'Connor* (1987) the court took a restrictive view of relevance, stating that the conviction of the other should only be admitted if it was a prerequisite to the convicting of the defendant. For example, in a handling case it would be permissible to prove the conviction of the other for theft, since this would establish the element of the offence for which the defendant was on trial, namely that the goods were stolen. *O'Connor* was a conspiracy case where the defendant was accused of conspiring to defraud with X in an insurance fraud. X pleaded guilty, but this should not have been admitted. In a two party conspiracy case, admitting the evidence of the guilty plea of one defendant would, by implication, point the finger at the other, and was too prejudicial and should be excluded under s 78 PACE 1984.

The narrow view that the conviction should be a condition precedent to the defendant's conviction was rejected in *R v Robertson* (1968) where the defendant was accused with two others of conspiracy. The guilty plea of one was held to be admissible, since it helped to show that there was a conspiracy. The prosecution would still need to show it was the defendant as opposed to any other who was involved. In this case the Court of Appeal expressed the view that s 74 should be used sparingly.

Likewise in *R v Lunnon* (1988) there was a multi-party conspiracy and the conviction of one of the parties was admissible to show that a conspiracy existed. There was no unfairness to the accused because it did not point the finger at his involvement. In *R v Bennett* (1979) the conviction of a shop girl for under-ringing the price of goods to give her friends cheap goods was admissible to show that there had been thefts from the supermarket. However, this did not point the finger at the defendant by implication, and was therefore admissible.

This needs to be contrasted with *R v Martin* (1990) where the conviction of X for indecency with another man, D, was inadmissible because the jury would certainly feel that the nature of such a crime pointed to D's guilt.

If the conviction is admissible then s 74(2) creates a statutory persuasive presumption that the conviction is correct unless the contrary is shown. It gives the party challenging the conviction the legal burden of proving it is wrong.

The convictions of the defendant

Section 74(3) deals with the defendant's convictions. As seen earlier in Chapter 5 on similar fact evidence, they are not normally relevant to prove his guilt. In the rare case where such convictions are relevant then s 74(3) operates as a statutory persuasive presumption with the burden of proof on the person denying the offence. If this is the prosecutor he or she must prove beyond reasonable doubt, whereas if it is the defendant the correct standard is balance of probability.

Where previous convictions are relevant under s 74, then the fact of conviction, and the contents of the indictment are admissible (s 75), and a certificate of conviction can be obtained (s 73). Nothing in s 74 renders admissible convictions of the defendant that would be inadmissible under the normal rules of evidence.

17 Public interest immunity and privilege

Introduction

In order for a court to reach the right decision in a case, all relevant and admissible evidence should be presented to the court. This ensures that there is efficient and fair administration of justice. However, there are cases where it may be considered desirable to withhold certain information, notwithstanding that it is relevant evidence. This may be because the public interest requires secrecy to be maintained, or because individual freedom or privileges need to be preserved. The issues of public interest immunity and privilege can occur in both civil and criminal cases and are determined by the courts by reference to certain principles which are outlined below.

Public interest immunity

In some cases the desirability of presenting all relevant information to the court must give way to a greater need to preserve secrecy and confidentiality, where disclosure would not be in the public interest. This raises the issue of public interest immunity, which can be claimed by the parties to the case, or a non-party who is being asked to supply certain information which they feel would be harmful to the public good if revealed.

The court must determine whether the claim to public interest immunity has any validity (*Conway v Rimmer* (1968)), although the court will usually be reluctant to investigate the claim of a government minister to public interest immunity, believing that the minister is usually in the best position to judge the nature of the information, especially where national security is involved: *Balfour v Foreign Office* (1993). Whether there will be any alteration in this practice following the Scott report on the Arms to Iraq enquiry remains to be seen.

Public interest immunity is often claimed where the information has national security implications, or involves high level affairs of state, or where the public interest requires protection of the source of information. Case law varies as to whether public interest immunity can be waived. In *Alfred Crompton Amusements v Commissioners for Customs and Excise* (1974) it was suggested that the person protected by the public interest immunity can waive it, whereas in *Rogers v Home Secretary* (1973) it was suggested that waiver is not possible.

If public interest immunity exists then the document itself cannot be revealed, and no secondary evidence is admissible either, which would reveal the contents of the document through a copy or oral evidence.

The test

Is the document likely to be necessary?

In order to test the public interest immunity claim, the court will hear argument from counsel as to the desirability of disclosing or withholding the information. At this stage the court does not look at the document in question, but tries to see whether there is evidence that the information is likely to be necessary for the fair disposing of the case or saving of costs (RSC Ord 24 r 13(1)), or is needed in the interests of justice in a criminal case. The courts will not permit 'fishing expeditions' where a party merely wants to see documents in the hope that they will reveal something useful, as in *Air Canada v Secretary of State for Trade (No 2)* (1983). In this case there was a dispute about landing charges at UK airports, and the plaintiff wanted to see government documents on public sector borrowing. The documents were not likely to be necessary, unlike in *Burmah Oil v Bank of England* (1980) where documents revealing the bank's policy and attitude in various documents relating to the company share sales were likely to be necessary to the plaintiff's case.

Are the documents actually necessary?

At this stage the judge will then look at the documents to see if they do actually contain material of use to the plaintiff although, if the documents are obviously high level national security or affairs of state, it is unlikely the judge will consider the documents. In *Campbell v Tameside* (1982) a school teacher had been attacked by a pupil and was suing her employers on the basis that they knew the child to be violent, and yet had placed him in normal schooling without adequate protection or a warning to the plaintiff. She sought disclosure of the authority's records, and the authority objected on the basis that such records should be confidential otherwise confidence and co-operation on the part of parents and children would cease. These documents were likely to be necessary and, having examined them, the court held that they were actually necessary. The test is whether the plaintiff has no chance of success without the documents but with them she has a chance, or that slim chances of success are transformed into stronger chances with the documents. The documents in *Burmah Oil* failed at this stage in that they were not actually necessary.

Balancing the competing interests

If the plaintiff manages to show that the documents are necessary then the court will need to balance the competing interests to see if disclosure should be ordered. There is the public interest in maintaining confidentiality, and the plaintiff's need to use the documents to stand a chance of winning his case. In *Campbell* the court said that once the documents were shown to be necessary, then there was a very heavy burden on the party wanting to withhold. Withholding the documents needs to be 'really necessary for the proper functioning of public service' (*Conway v Rimmer*), rather than necessary to save the embarrassment of the person seeking to withhold.

Types of public interest immunity claims

The courts have tended to draw a distinction between 'class claims' and 'contents claims'. A class claim is where withholding is argued to be necessary because the document, regardless of its actual contents, belongs to a class of document that should not be disclosed. A contents claim is based on the fact that the document's actual contents would be damaging to the public good if revealed. It is often easier to justify a so called contents claim, but the distinction should not be taken as an automatic guide to whether disclosure will be ordered or not; it will all depend on the facts of the case (*R v Chief Constable of West Midlands, ex p Wiley* (1994)).

High level affairs of state and national security

The high level workings of government, both within the UK and in its diplomacy overseas will almost always be protected from disclosure: *Balfour v Foreign Office; Burmah Oil v Bank of England*. With national security claims the court is mindful of the damage disclosure could cause, and it is common to withhold such information, as in *Duncan v Cammel Laird* (1942) where the plaintiff sought plans of a submarine still in active service. This would not be justified if the information was already in the public domain because, for example, the submarine was open to the public or was being sold extensively to other countries at arms fairs worldwide.

Local government and bodies with delegated authority

Many local authorities perform functions of public importance where confidentiality is essential to maintain public confidence in the system and to ensure it functions properly. Where a good claim to confidentiality can be made out then there will be no disclosure, as in *D v NSPCC* (1978) concerning the identity of an informant in a child abuse case. However, as can be seen from *Campbell* disclosure may sometimes be ordered.

Complaints and grievance procedures

It is often argued that the proper functioning of complaints and grievance procedures requires confidentiality and that, as the statements are made to bodies responsible for the investigation of such complaints, the documents should not be disclosed. In *Neilson v Laugharne* (1981) such complaints to the police complaints procedure were held to be subject to public interest immunity. However, this is no longer automatic (*R v Chief Constable of West Midlands, ex p Wiley* (1995), overruling *Neilson*), and will depend on the contents of the documents in question. However, there will still be public interest immunity in relation to the working papers of officers investigating complaints: *Taylor v Anderton* (1995).

Detection and prevention of crime

The police depend upon information from informants in the fight against crime. Such informants would be unwilling to come forward and help the police if they thought that their identity would be disclosed. In *Marks v Beyfus* (1890) it was acknowledged that the identity of an informant would normally be the proper subject of a public interest immunity claim. However, the public interest in maintaining secrecy would give way if the identity of the informant was necessary to help establish the innocence of the accused. This may arise if there is evidence that the informant may have participated in or committed the crime in question, or was motivated by a grudge against the accused. This does not apply just to informants in criminal cases; it can apply in child abuse cases (*D v NSPCC* (1978)), or tax or customs cases: *Alfred Crompton Amusements v Commissioners of Customs and Excise* (1974).

The protection given to informants provides the basis for a public interest immunity claim in respect of identifying premises used for police surveillance or observation: *R v Rankine* (1986). If disclosure were allowed it could undermine the efficiency of operations, deter occupiers from allowing the use of their premises, and lead to threats, violence or harassment. Disclosure will be ordered if it is necessary to prevent a miscarriage of justice, and if there is opposition to disclosure then the police must give evidence in court as to the attitude of the occupier to disclosure, and any difficulties disclosure could cause: *R v Johnson* (1968). If there is no objection by the occupier, or no occupier to be concerned about, then disclosure will be ordered: *R v Brown* and *R v Daley* (1988). It is not sufficient for the police to argue that the efficiency of their surveillance post will be affected.

Confidentiality

There is no routine public interest immunity just because the information was supplied in confidence: *Alfred Crompton Amusements* (1974). It will all depend on the circumstances of the case and whether the public interest in preserving and recognising confidentiality outweighs the individual's need to know. The doctor/patient relationship, the priest and penitent do not have absolute confidentiality guaranteed. In *AG v*

Mulholland (1963) Lord Denning said that there was no automatic public interest immunity, but that there would need to be compelling reasons before the court would require disclosure.

In *Science Research Council v Nasse* (1980) the plaintiffs sought disclosure of their fellow employees' confidential personnel records to try to show discrimination in the workplace. The House of Lords refused disclosure, holding that the public interest in such records remaining confidential outweighed the individual need for the documents.

Privilege

A claim to privilege is justified by reference to a right or interest that an individual has in maintaining the secrecy or confidentiality of the information concerned. There is no wide concept of privilege in English law; instead the party claiming privilege must bring their case within one of the recognised categories.

Privilege can be waived by the individual entitled to the protection it confers, and such waiver may be deliberate or accidental. However, if the waiver occurs through fraud or a lawyer's obvious mistake then this does not count as waiver: *Guinness Peat Properties v Fitzroy Robinson Partnership* (1987). If privileged is waived it is not possible to limit it to some parts of the document only, unless the parts of the document relate to different matters and can be severed: *Great Atlantic Assurance Co v Home Insurance* (1981).

Where privilege exists this only extends to the original document, not secondary evidence by way of a copy of the contents or oral evidence from someone who has seen the document: *Calcraft v Guest* (1898). However, if it is discovered in time that the opponent has secondary evidence of privileged documents, then the use of secondary evidence can be prevented by injunction (*Lord Ashburton v Pape* (1913)), regardless of whether there was impropriety or not (*Goddard v Nationwide Building Society* (1986)).

The privilege against self-incrimination

A defendant cannot refuse to answer questions that incriminate him in respect of the offence charged: s 1(e) Criminal Evidence Act 1898. However, it may be possible for the defendant and other witnesses to refuse to answer questions that may incriminate them in relation to an offence for which they are not presently on trial. This is the privilege against self-incrimination, and means that such questions may go unanswered. If they are answered in an incriminatory way, the answers could be used against the witness in subsequent criminal proceedings since they would amount to an admission.

The privilege against self-incrimination applies if answering the question either directly or indirectly incriminates the witness (*Rank Film Distributors v Video Information Centre* (1982)), where the answer would have led to the recovery of incriminatory evidence. Incriminating the witness means to expose him to the risk of criminal proceedings in the UK or to European Community sanctions or penalties: *Rio Tinto Zinc v Westinghouse* (1978). It does not extend to possible civil proceedings, nor does it extend to the risk of proceedings in foreign courts. This is expressly provided for in civil cases by s 14 Civil Evidence Act 1968, and, given that it would be very difficult to assess the risk of foreign proceedings, the same rule should apply in criminal cases.

There has to be a real and substantial risk of exposing the witness to future criminal proceedings (*Rio Tinto Zinc*) by the answering of the question. If the witness is already facing such charges, or has given the information already, then there is no privilege. The risk must be more than fanciful; it must be real. It would be necessary to take into account the attitude of the prosecution authorities, the length of time, the seriousness of the offence, the strength of the case, etc, as to whether there is a substantial risk of proceedings being brought. Remember if an accused has already been acquitted or convicted of the offence in relation to which he is asked questions, there is no privilege, since he cannot be prosecuted for the same offence twice. Nor can a child under 10 claim the privilege, since they cannot be prosecuted for a crime.

The privilege extends to questions that would incriminate the witness or their spouse in civil cases: s 14(1) Civil Evidence Act 1968. The position has not been expressed in criminal cases, and so it is unclear whether the privilege extends to spouses.

If the witness is wrongly made to answer a question in respect of which they should have been allowed a privilege, then the answer is inadmissible in subsequent criminal proceedings: *R v Garbett* (1847).

Exceptions to the privilege
Where a privilege exists there is the possibility that the witness will be deprived of it by the operation of statutory rules. The following are examples.
- Supreme Court Act 1981 s 72
  In intellectual property cases, where there are allegations such as infringement of copyright, the witness cannot refuse to answer questions on the basis of incriminating themselves or their spouse.

However, the answers are inadmissible in any subsequent criminal proceedings save for perjury or contempt.

- Theft Act 1968 s 31
  Where a witness is asked questions relating to execution of a trust, accounts for property, administration of property, etc, the privilege against self-incrimination or incriminating a spouse is lost. However, as above, the answer is inadmissible in subsequent criminal proceedings under the Act against the witness or spouse.

- Children Act 1989 s 98
  The privilege against incriminating oneself or spouse is lost in proceedings under the Act relating to the care, supervision and protection of a child. However, the answers are inadmissible in subsequent criminal proceedings.

- Criminal Justice Act 1987 s 2
  In cases involving serious fraud investigations individuals are forced to answer questions as there have been a number of statutory provisions taking away the privilege to self-incrimination. This was the situation involving Ernest Saunders in the Guinness fraud cases.

Legal professional privilege

The *first limb* of legal professional privilege covers communication between a client and his legal adviser, which is in the usual course of legal practice. This can cover the giving of advice and information. There is no need for matters to involve litigation, although clearly the privilege exists in relation to litigious matters also. The legal adviser can be a barrister, solicitor, or legal adviser in paid employment provided that they act in their capacity as legal adviser: *Minter v Priest* (1930).

The privilege covers 'communication'. It does not prevent a lawyer from having to give evidence about his own observations of facts, nor can items or documents merely be given to a solicitor for safe keeping to attract privilege.

The privilege can be lost if the purpose was to further a crime or a fraud, rather than merely giving advice as to whether particular behaviour would be a crime. The intention to further a fraud or crime may be that of the client, the solicitor or a third party. In *R v Central Criminal Court ex p Francis* (1989) disclosure of communication between a solicitor and his client in relation to a conveyancing matter was ordered as the normal privilege had been lost because a third party (the nephew of the client) had supplied the funds used in order to launder money from drugs offences.

The *second limb* of legal professional privilege attaches to communication between the lawyer and a third party, or the client and a third party. Litigation has to be contemplated or pending for there to be such a privilege: *Wheeler v Le Marchant*. It is then necessary to show that the litigation was the dominant purpose behind the communication: *Waugh v British Railways Board* (1980). In this case communications between one of the parties and safety experts after a rail crash was not privileged. Although litigation was a prospect, it was not the dominant purpose of the report, which was to find out what went wrong, so that safety could be improved and future accidents avoided.

As before, the privilege can be lost if the communication was to further a crime or fraud. This limb may also be lost in cases involving welfare of children if the interests of the child require disclosure: *Re L (a minor) (Police Investigations)* (1996). However first limb privilege is not lost on this basis.

There is no loss of either type of legal professional privilege just because disclosure would avoid injustice to an accused. In *R v Derby Magistrates' Court ex p B* (1995) a defendant failed in his attempt to get disclosure of statements made by another man to his solicitors that implicated the other man and exonerated the accused in the offence charged. In this case, the court overruled the earlier cases of *R v Ataou* (1988) and *R v Barton* (1973) in which this had been suggested.

It follows therefore that legal professional privilege is that of the client and will continue until he waives it or loses it for some other reason. It does not matter that the client no longer benefits from the privilege. Items subject to legal professional privilege cannot be seized by the police (s 10 PACE 1984), unless the privilege has been lost.

Limited journalistic privilege

Section 10 Contempt of Court Act 1981 gives journalists a limited privilege and means that they do not have to reveal their sources of information unless disclosure is necessary in the interests of justice, national security or prevention of crime and disorder.

The person seeking disclosure has the burden of proving disclosure is necessary for one of the stated reasons. 'Necessary' was given a strict meaning of 'essential' in *Maxwell v Pressdram* (1987), although in *Re An Inquiry Under the Companies Security (Insider Dealing) Act 1985* a lower standard of 'very useful' was applied.

Material subject to journalistic privilege cannot be seize by the police without a warrant and order from a circuit judge: ss 11–14 PACE.

167

Without prejudice communications

There is no legal professional privilege that covers communications between parties to an action. However, if such communication is a genuine attempt to reach a settlement then it can attract a privilege. Such communications are termed 'without prejudice' and cannot be disclosed in court, or taken as an admission of guilt.

Merely labelling a letter 'without prejudice' does not create the privilege; it is the intention to reach a settlement that does: *Rush & Tompkins v GLC* (1988). Documents and oral conversations can be privileged under this heading, and the privilege can only be waived with both parties' agreement.

The privilege continues even after the litigation ends or is settled, although the parties themselves can use the communication to prove that agreement was reached, and on the matter of costs. Such a letter would be a *Calderbank* letter and by RSC Ord 22 r 14 it can be referred to determine costs, provided that there was no opportunity to protect the party's position by payment into court. Thus a *Calderbank* letter may have the effect of making the opponent liable for costs from the date of the letter if he fails to recover more at trial than the letter offered.

Index